CUMBRIA AT WAR

CUMBRIA AT WAR

1939–1945

Ron Freethy

COUNTRYSIDE BOOKS
NEWBURY BERKSHIRE

First published 2009

COUNTRYSIDE BOOKS
3 Catherine Road
Newbury, Berkshire

To view our complete range of books, please visit us at
www.countrysidebooks.co.uk

ISBN 978 1 84674 158 6

Produced through MRM Associates Ltd., Reading
Typeset by CJWT Solutions, St Helens
Printed by Cambridge University Press

All material for the manufacture of this book was sourced from sustainable forests.

Contents

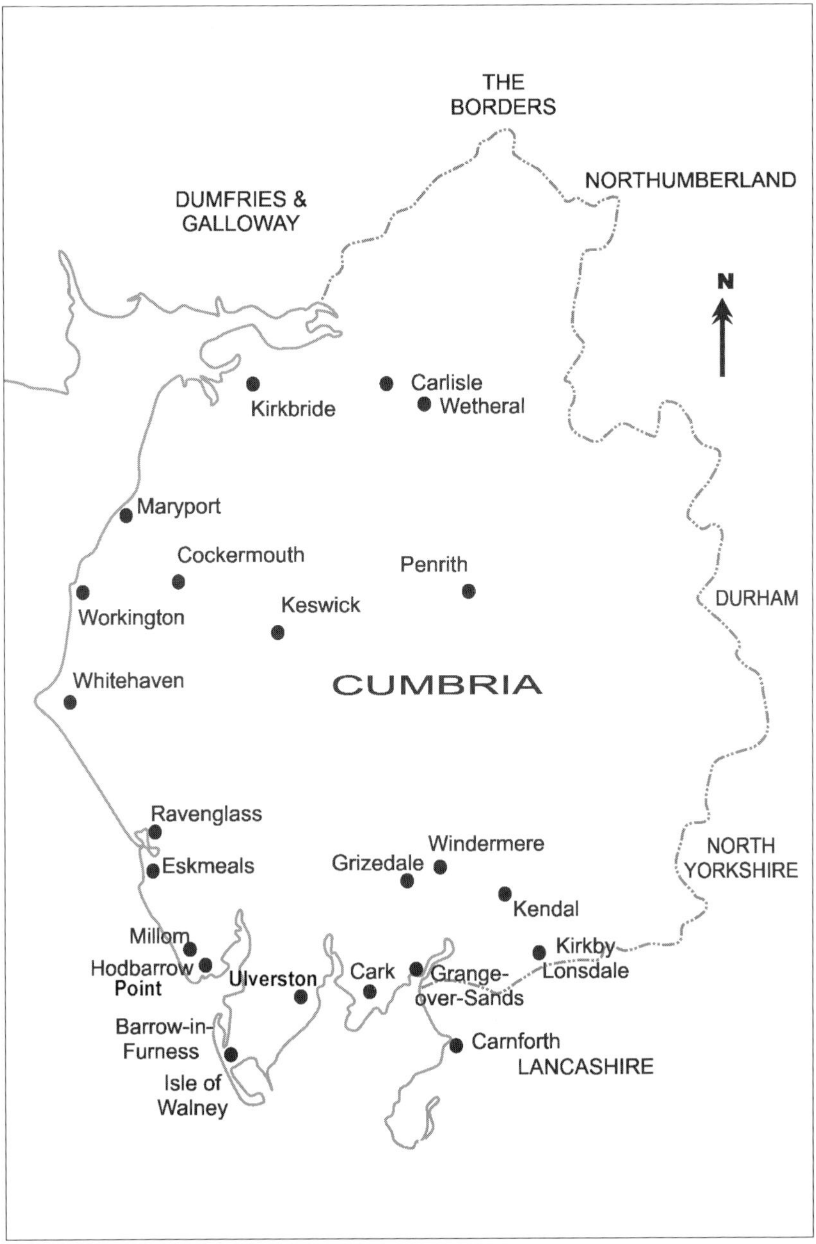
THE BORDERS
DUMFRIES & GALLOWAY
NORTHUMBERLAND
N
Carlisle
Kirkbride
Wetheral
Maryport
Cockermouth
Penrith
Workington
Keswick
DURHAM
Whitehaven
CUMBRIA
Ravenglass
Windermere
Eskmeals
Grizedale
NORTH YORKSHIRE
Kendal
Millom
Kirkby Lonsdale
Hodbarrow Point
Ulverston
Cark
Grange-over-Sands
Barrow-in-Furness
Carnforth
LANCASHIRE
Isle of Walney

Introduction

When I started to research this book I was well aware that some folk, who were present in Cumbria during the war, would point out that the title could not be right.

Let me explain. With the county boundary changes of 1974 a new county of Cumbria was formed. This was made up of the Furness area of north-west Lancashire, the county of Westmorland with its chief administrative centre at Appleby, and the county of Cumberland with the focus of operations in Carlisle. 'Cumbria at War' is far more manageable a title than 'North Lancashire, Cumberland and Westmorland at War'!

People from the south of England may well believe that Cumbria was too isolated to be involved in the war at all. This was not so, because an invasion from the south-east would almost certainly have been supported by Nazi troops from Southern Ireland landing along the Cumbrian coast, where there were substantial harbours at Barrow, Millom, Ravenglass, Whitehaven, Workington and Maryport.

This book will trace the period between 1938 and 1946 and use the words of people who were there to ensure that these tough but momentous years are not forgotten.

I was born in Barrow-in-Furness in 1936 close to the docks and, as a four-year-old, I remember moving into the countryside after the blitz, and watching with interest as evacuees from a foreign land called Salford tried to settle in.

I remember watching aircraft practising bombing around our once quiet beach and the Americans coming to do some training on waste land near our house prior to setting off for Normandy in 1944.

My researches have been helped by a number of school

friends who shared my memories. Every author needs help from friends and in this respect I have been lucky. In particular, I wish to thank Brian McMullen of the Forestry Commission, who was a constant source of ideas and provided me with other contacts and Geoff Cain, whose wartime diaries and deep knowledge of the area have been invaluable. Of course there will be omissions, because some of the work was secret and there will be memories of which I am unaware. These memories could be written down and sent to me or better still sent to the local library.

I also wish to thank my wife Marlene, whose technical skills in the preparation of the manuscript far surpass my own, and also my publishers. As usual they have provided ideas, guidance and the editorial skills needed to produce this book.

The new county of Cumbria should be proud of the role, both secret and routine, which it played in the Second World War.

Ron Freethy

Chapter 1

Secrets, Spies and Starfish

In the mid to late 1930s Cumbria should be regarded as the 'place of spies'. The coast was still reached by only one road and one rail-link, both very vulnerable in the event of war. One would think that the area would not be one to attract tourists. Why then should the Cumbrian coast be so popular with German tourists and why should the German Zeppelin *Hindenburg* fly over Barrow in the mid-1930s on what was described as a 'courtesy visit'? These aerial tourists, armed with a battery of cameras, were said to be fascinated by the Vickers shipyard and the docks. There are eye-witnesses who can remember the airship flying so low that they were able to wave at and shout to the Germans on board.

Furthermore, many of the pleasure steamers that cruised around the north-west coast had English names, but were

PORTENTS OF WAR

The Hindenburg *flying over Barrow in the 1930s. It was on a so-called 'goodwill mission' and contained affluent Germans waving to people below and taking hundreds of photographs. (The Dock Museum, Barrow-in-Furness)*

owned by German companies and were often crewed by Germans! The plot really did thicken, as was brought home to me when reading my diaries written in the 1970s after talking to relatives. Many members of my family worked in the post offices around Cumbria and especially in Barrow.

My godmother, Miss Doris Dickenson, was the postmistress at the Michaelson Road office, close to the docks. She was a devout Christian who saw 'good in every soul' but even she was sceptical of the German presence and recalled: 'Oh yes – you could see that the German threat was building. In 1934 there were no German visitors posting letters home but by 1937 there were so many tourists who all seemed to be very well off, spoke perfect English and stayed longer than would have been the case with normal tourists. There was a flood of letters on most days but, surprisingly, few postcards, which were obviously open to view. Some of these tourists hired motorcycles and cars to enjoy educational tours of the area. At one time maps were ordered in bulk from the bookshops, which actually ran out of copies. The tourists were always ready to talk to the ship workers and buy them drinks in the local pubs.'

All these activities obviously came to the notice of the authorities, but there was not a lot that could be done about it in peacetime. What was done, however, was to ask locals to beware of giving away sensitive material relating to their workplace and to tell people how to spot a spy. This I learned when I talked to Ted Cowlishaw, who was a postman in Barrow: 'We were told to look out for accents which were not local and to talk to them using local dialect. The Germans could never use or pronounce the word "marra", meaning a friend, and neither could they understand the details of Rugby League players or the names of the Hound Trail winners of the past.'

Later, it was thought that local communists might also disrupt the war effort and in June 1940 the council in Barrow debated whether to sack a librarian who was a pacifist and was

During the 1930s two bus companies operated in Cumbria. The first was run (perhaps significantly) by Johann W. Kaiser, seen to the left of this picture. Kaiser Wilhelm II gave a Mercedes car to Lord Lonsdale (seen right). From 1911 Kaiser ran a bicycle firm and motor business based in Keswick.

distributing copies of the *Daily Worker* during her lunch breaks.

The German 'tourists' did not confine their visits to Barrow and made good use of two companies who were running escorted tours into Cumbria during the 1930s. One was owned by Johann Kaiser, who had come to England in 1909 to be the chauffeur of a new Mercedes car given to Lord Lonsdale of Lowther Hall by none other than Kaiser Wilhelm II. Johann set up a cycle business in Keswick in 1911 and developed this into a thriving coach business by the mid 1920s. With that name, no wonder the Keswick tours were attractive to the German tourists.

They also patronised William Sim's company, which ran trips from his open-topped 1930 vintage Chevrolet and other

William Sim operated a tourist service with this open-top Chevrolet in the 1930s, along with other vehicles. German 'tourists' were among his most frequent passengers.

vehicles, many of the tourists making extensive notes and taking photographs. There was also interest in the Ravenglass and Eskdale narrow-gauge railway known to the locals as 'Ratty'. This would be closed to passenger traffic for the duration of the war but the Germans were aware of the value of the local quarries and of this quick access for invading troops seeking out potential resistance fighters.

Not all the locals welcomed this influx of bogus tourists, as Elsie Proctor told me in 2008: 'One of my uncles was convinced that he may have hindered the work of some spies. He was a driver on Ratty and in 1937 he noticed a group of German tourists photographing the line and the views over the estuary. The Germans were still at it as time approached for the last train of the day. They were the only ones in view high on

Ratty at Boot Station with the engine Collossus *in 1920.*

the hills and he knew what the buggers were like for timetables. So he left five minutes early without sounding the traditional warning hoot. For all he knew they might be up there still and he laughed at this until the day he died in 1982.'

The German threat, especially to Barrow, meant that one very positive move was made. Plans were drawn up, printed and distributed to those who 'needed to know'. I have a copy of the Barrow Protection Plan dated 1940 and signed by the Naval Officer in Charge. His signature was deliberately blurred in order to keep his identity a secret. Reading this report it can be appreciated just how important Barrow was and why the German spies were so hard at work. The report, included here in full, makes chilling reading.

The Importance of Defending Barrow-in-Furness

In my judgment, were Barrow to fall into the hands of the enemy, even for a brief period, the results accruing from such enemy occupation would be as follows:-

(a) ***It would constitute a major naval disaster.***
To appreciate the position it must be realised that there is not only a considerable fleet of warships actually building at Barrow, but gun mountings and in some cases guns, for primary, secondary and tertiary armaments in battleships, cruisers and destroyers building in other yards, and director towers essential to the fire control arrangements of ALL new naval constructions are in hand.

To put the matter in a nutshell, since ships are useless without guns, re-enforcements to the fleet at a time when expansion of our naval power is vital, might be indefinitely withheld. This applies to the following numbers and classes of vessels:

4 Battleships
9 Cruisers (including two building at Barrow)
7 Destroyers
25 Submarines (all building at Barrow)
1 Aircraft carrier (building at Barrow)
5 Destroyers whose engines are being built at Barrow and their hulls on Tyne
2 Turkish Destroyers
4 Turkish Submarines
2 15" gun mountings for defence of the Dardanelles

(b) ***The expansion of the R.A.F. would be seriously retarded.***

1. *From the reserve fuel tanks at Barrow, twelve million gallons of aviation spirit would be appropriated or destroyed.*

2. *The whole of the requirements of forged steel aero engine cylinders for the main Bristol and shadow* *factories are being undertaken by Vickers Armstrong Ltd, Barrow. There are now two types using forged steel cylinders or sleeves and the rate of delivery is 3,000 per week, which will be ultimately increased to 4,000. Barrow is the only factory having the necessary machinery for dealing with the exceptionally tough steel used in this work and as probably most of these engines are 8 cylinder, the significance of this work does not require to be emphasised.*

3. Wooden parts for all the aircraft being built at the Chester and Blackpool works affiliated to Vickers are being provided from Barrow. The rate of delivery is 25 sets per week which will be increased to 30-35 in the near future. If this supply should be cut off, delivery of planes from these factories would cease.

4. Undercarriages for Wellington, Hurricane and Blenheim bombers are under construction to the extent, at the moment, of 180 sets. This work is continuing.

(c) ***The provision of A/A guns for the Army would be affected to a minor extent.***
The following A/A construction for the War Office is in hand:

2 in No. 3.7 mobile equipments
24 in No. 3.7 static mountings
15 in No. 4.5 H/A/LA mountings

Finally, an immense amount of damage could be done to the docks by the simple expedient of removing all dock and lock gates on an ebb tide. The entire system would violently empty itself. Relieved of water pressure, the dock wells would cave in, cranes probably following them over the side, and vessels in the fitting out berth would ground in a state of confusion. The damage resulting would take at least two years to make good, the port being immobilised for the time being for the fitting out of ships of any kind.

Now that a 6" gun battery has been mounted at Hilpsford Point, I do not anticipate a frontal attack on the port but troops could be landed on the foreshore on Walney Is at points not covered by the fixed defences. Alternatively, a landing could be made on either flank in the near vicinity on sands which dry out at low water, by aircraft or shallow draft vessels, the latter approaching the coast at the top of high water, grounding on the falling tide and hoisting out tanks, artillery, etc., using their own gear. A large proportion of the existing garrison is manning the fixed defences and owing to shortage of small arms would have little opportunity of self-defence from attack from the rear.

2nd July, 1940
Naval Officer in Charge
Barrow-in-Furness

The reference made in this report to the presence of vital fuel dumps did not just apply to Barrow. There were other storage facilities all over Cumbria but especially near to the airfields at Cark, Millom, Kirkbride and others. There were also supplies hidden close to the ports of Ravenglass, Whitehaven, Workington and Maryport.

Because of the threat of a German invasion of the north-west coast from Southern Ireland, plans were drawn up to be distributed to all relevant personnel should troop movements be imminent, including the police who would co-ordinate the plan in association with the Home Guard, fire services, hospitals, air raid wardens, women's voluntary groups and others who could play a useful role.

There had to be a Command Structure with telephone links and a secure place built underground to ensure that everything was co-ordinated. The essential personnel had to be vetted, required to sign the Official Secrets Act and be trained. Furthermore, plans had to be drawn up to protect vital installations including water supplies. Particular attention was focussed on the 90-mile underground pipeline, which led from the Thirlmere area to most of the Lancashire towns en route to Manchester. Without the water industry the war effort would have ground to a halt. In 2005, I made a series of radio documentaries following this pipeline, which was built in Victorian times, and I had to be careful not to disclose vulnerable points that could still be the target for terrorist attacks.

These so-called War Rooms were vital and were present not only in Barrow but also in other major Cumbrian towns. The Naval Officer's report mentioned above lists not just ships but large guns as a major product of the Vickers yard. These had to be tested and this was done on the sand dune system near Ravenglass at Eskmeals. It should be repeated that the German 'tourists' were keen to photograph the Roman port of Ravenglass. Or were they? The guns and the ammunition for the guns were transported by rail and very secret plans were needed to ensure that both the rail route and the firing range were given maximum protection. Even today the area is still designated as a '*danger spot*' and is so marked on the OS and road maps.

In the 1930s, guns and ammunition were pulled from the railway sidings to the firing positions by horses and this was the case until the end of the war. All the men who worked on the range, even those with many years' service, were carefully vetted and were obliged to carry extra identification. Guards were placed in the area.

Finding these secret plans requires some effort as the thick dust of history begins to settle and locating people who worked in these areas is obviously becoming more difficult as time moves on. I was lucky to find two men who were both aware, if for different reasons, of the secret work which was going on during the war. These stalwarts were John Davies and Jimmy Weatherburn.

John Davies spent all of his working life repairing and studying radio transmitters: 'My bosses knew at least from 1935 that us and Jerry were involved in serious research on radio beams. Even then the boffins knew about very high frequency (VHF) radio signals and the RADAR was a similar sort of echo location to that used by bats. We also knew that these transmissions could be interfered with or even blocked. We had to keep a record of everybody who had a high powered radio transmitter and we were warned about spies. We were given a poster pointing out that "Tittle Tattle Lost the Battle" and for a while we had visions of a spy

As early as 1890 the Eskmeals gun range was a secret place. When this photograph was taken in the mid-1920s, the photographer must have had special permission. Horses were used to drag guns into position prior to test firing and this was the case until well into the Second World War.

dressed in black and carrying a smoking bomb around every corner.'

There is no doubt that not all the German 'tourists' went home before the start of hostilities – there must have been so-called 'sleepers' who had forged papers and lots of money. Many would have had 'wives' with them who were also trained to pick up any relevant 'Tittle Tattle'.

Jimmy Weatherburn takes up the secret story: 'At the start of the war I was just finishing my apprenticeship at the Vickers-Armstrong shipyard when I was sent into an office and asked a lot of personal questions. Two days later I was told to sign the Official Secrets Act, had my photograph taken for a pass which would let me in to a secret area. I thought at the time that I was specially good at my job and I hope nearly 70 years later that this was true. I was, however, nobbut a little chap and I was soon working in a cramped cigar-shaped box which turned out

Jimmy Weatherburn who helped to build the Midget submarines during the Second World War.

A Midget submarine being lowered into the water.

to be the centre section of what became known as an X craft midget submarine. A small fleet of these were built in Barrow and in 1943 their brave four-man crew helped to immobilize the German battleship *Tirpitz*. These craft were later featured in the film *Above Us The Waves* starring John Mills. He looked brave enough but not so brave as those lads I met whilst the X boats were on their trials. Each sub was built in three sections which we had to rivet and bolt together. We knew that our work had to be spot on or the crew operating them would die.

'Underwater there were batteries but on the surface there was a diesel engine. I'll bet you will be surprised to know that the engine was the same as that used to power a London double-decker bus. The engine worked a treat but the clutch presented a problem and my boss and I were sent to the crews' training

The periscope of an 'X' Craft submarine made in Barrow. (The Dock Museum, Barrow-in-Furness)

base in Scotland to make adjustments. We obviously had to work at top speed but while we were there we ate the same food as the crew. We had a breakfast of two eggs, bacon, sausage with proper meat in it and white bread. At night we enjoyed proper steak. What a change from our rations at home but the Navy lads were risking their lives each and every day even when only engaged in trials and they deserved each and every crumb. At this time we were aware of the need for secrecy and none of us told anybody where we had been or what we were doing. We knew we could help to win the war by keeping our mouths tight shut.'

Apart from a limited number of photographs, few memories remain of the X craft but in the Dock Museum in Barrow there is a good example of a midget submarine's periscope and details of its finely-engineered structure can clearly be seen.

There were other even more dangerous experiments which preceded the invention of the X craft and these were referred to as 'chariots'. The crew of two rode astride the so-called chariots which submerged with their brave passengers enveloped in diving gear. They then attached limpet mines to the hull of ships. Graham Cubbin who works at the Dock Museum told me: 'We have a smashing slice of archive material relating to the charioteers, one of whom was a Barrow lad. He was James Freel and he mounted his chariot and entered the waters beneath Palermo Harbour and placed his mines which destroyed some of the Italian Fleet in 1940. There is a photograph of the decorated James Freel along with his mother and father during a period of well-earned leave.'

Everyone knew that our Cumbrian ports and flat beaches were vulnerable to invading troops and huge blocks of timber were placed in the shallows to keep the enemy from getting too close and to provide an opportunity to kill them if they did manage to wade ashore. There would certainly be bombing prior to any invasion. The Vickers yard would be top of the Luftwaffe 'hit list' but they also knew of the steel works and iron-ore mines which were features of not only the Barrow area

The 'Chariot hero' James Freel on leave in Barrow with his proud parents.

but also around Millom, Whitehaven, Workington and Maryport.

However, even though the enemy knew where these installations were they still had to hit the target and so blackout procedures were rigorously enforced whilst even more subtle and secret plans were developed. Reliable building firms were contacted and sworn to secrecy. They were involved in what became known as *Operation Starfish*.

The building firms were instructed to build new 'houses'. These were only made of wood and had nothing inside them and from the air they looked like dock installations. When German bombers were in the area, a barrage of shells was fired from the bogus village and the occasional light was deliberately leaked. Only a very few people knew of the 'New Walney Village' which was set on the edge of Hilpsford Point. The electrical firm of Hartley and Bramhall was obliged to sign the

Official Secrets Act and to lay electrical cables to light up the 'Starfish Subterfuge'. Very little remains today as the spoof lies beneath a huge colony of nesting seagulls on the popular South Walney Nature Reserve. A look at a map of Barrow shows that Walney is an island separated from the main town by the High Level and Low Level bridges. There is an obvious indentation which divides the island into a north side and a south side. It was clear that the Starfish construction had to be at the southern end because it was nearest to the dock complex and, in any case, there was a military airfield to the north of the island.

The Walney airfield complex was developing quickly and eventually had 1,500 service men and women, plus civilian support staff. It was a base for the training of air gunners. First Lysanders and then Defiants towed targets called 'drogues' and gunners practised shooting them down. Later, Ansons were

The site of the 'Starfish' mock-up on Walney Island today. It is now a bird reserve overlooking Piel Castle.

used as they could take more than two trainees at a time. At the end of the war Wellingtons were brought into use. Barrow and Barnes Wallis had come full circle. The airfield was close to the old airship base where Wallis trained and it was he who used similar techniques in his design of the Wellington.

Because the Western Lake District has always been difficult to access (which is why it has been so popular) several secret meetings were held there prior to, during and even after the war. Many of these meetings were never recorded for obvious reasons, but I have located one that was of major importance. This was held at Killoran House, in the village of Wetheral, near Carlisle. This is now a pleasant tea room also offering accommodation but until the 1960s it was owned by Rolls-Royce. In 2004 I had the privilege of talking to Fred Morley who was part of the design team working with Frank Whittle to develop the jet engine.

Fred recalled: 'First we were moved from Derby and then to a secret location in an old cotton mill near Clitheroe. This was obviously further away from the bombing and I've never worked so bloody hard in all my life. The whole team loved being stretched to the limit and we were as mad as hell when pin-striped hooligans from Whitehall sent us up to Killoran House to report on progress. Why the buggers did not come to see the engine itself still beats me. They would not have been impressed because to start with the thing looked like a pile of milk churns bolted together. Anyway, it used to take us three days to get there and back via the Settle to Carlisle railway. We could have used the time better by getting on with the work. All we did was eat well, drink even better and try to explain how the engine worked by showing drawings to a bunch of bloody civil servants with no engineering background. I remember one meeting when Frank Whittle himself was present. Frank could be an awkward bugger and I can't say I blamed him. He had the original idea which did not appeal to the Air Ministry. So he went out and funded it himself in his spare time. Once the engine looked like working

Frank Whittle (right) with Rolls-Royce executive, John Herriot.

he was reminded that he was a serving officer and could not share in the profits. These were to be divided between Rolls-Royce and the Government. You asked me about secrets during the war. What has still to be a well-kept secret is Frank Whittle's language when he was told to keep working but he would get nowt! Killoran has heard nothing like this before or since!'

There are many other secrets of Cumbria which will almost certainly never be fully unravelled. It is known that an inventory was drawn up of all the big houses and stately homes in Cumbria. It was certain that these would be commandeered by high-ranking German officers should the invasion succeed and Britain become occupied. Hit groups made up of explosive experts, plus those who knew the areas, who worked in the local mines and quarries, were told how to blow up these houses and how to place booby traps.

There were also plans to blow up iron ore and coal mines, some of which had workings tunnelled beneath the sea. Special Home Guard units, who were fitter and more adaptable than most, were set up as hit squads to disrupt port installations and road junctions. Winston Churchill's words, 'We shall fight in the hills' were particularly relevant to Cumbria.

There were also other small but nevertheless significant events taking place in Cumbria, not least the work being carried out at Coniston on the *Bluebird* project.

In 2008 I had a long and fascinating conversation with Vicki Slowe, the curator of the Ruskin Museum in Coniston, which now houses the Donald Campbell archives and what remains of the wreck of *Bluebird*. The workshop where *Bluebird* was based still stands and is close to the berth of the steam-powered tourist attraction vessel called *The Gondola*. I'm told by people who were living in Coniston at the time that, during the late 1930s, German tourists were often seen marvelling at *Bluebird*.

Vicki Slowe takes up the story: 'When you look at photographs of *Bluebird* at full speed it does look more like an aeroplane than a conventional boat. This is proved not only by the streamlined shape but also by the tailfin. Actually "make do and mend" was not just a wartime slogan – the *Bluebird* team had no money to spare after the war and the boat's tail fin was actually an aircraft's tail end. Donald Campbell also spent some time before and during the war at the Samlesbury Engineering Company situated between Preston and Blackburn. He was shown how to tune up engines to make his speedboats go even faster. What the *Bluebird* team were doing in the war was designing Motor Torpedo Boats (MTBs). The

Germans were also experimenting with their high speed E boats and, during 1937 and 1938, Campbell's every move was shadowed by a retinue of spies but the locals do seem to have kept one step ahead and most of their secrets remained secure. Research into designs and engines went on throughout the war but the obvious focus was not on *Bluebird* itself but on the war effort. There was, however, a spin-off which helped Donald set up many water speed records just after the war. It is not just Vera Lynn's bluebirds over the white cliffs of Dover which should have a part in the history of World War Two, Campbell's *Bluebird* deserves a lot more than just a passing mention.'

I spent some time in the Air Force on Malta during the late 1950s and the MTBs were still doing sterling service in the Mediterranean. Norman Simpson, who served aboard MTBs during the war, told me: 'The boats were just huge with massive engines and fuel tanks that left little room for comfort. We knew we were sitting on a bomb but when we collected a shot-down airman from the sea we were all grateful that these boats could move away from danger at high speed.'

Geoff Cain recalls: 'Obviously I was not aware of the contribution made by the *Bluebird* team during the war but there was lots of secret stuff going on at Vickers. There was one rumour going round that they were building concrete boats and it seems that so were the Germans. These were sort of floating pillboxes which were placed at vulnerable places on canals and rivers. I heard that the Germans used them to guard bridges during our invasion at Arnhem in Holland.'

When visiting Holland in 2007 I was told of two of these concrete boats which were still present on the river Rhine, near Amsterdam, and which had been converted into houseboats. It took just a little effort to find one and despite the wooden living space on top, the military strength below was still very obvious.

What has also become obvious as I researched this chapter was that so many of the secrets must have been lost forever.

The Bluebird *K4 that Malcolm Campbell broke the speed record with at Coniston in August 1939.*

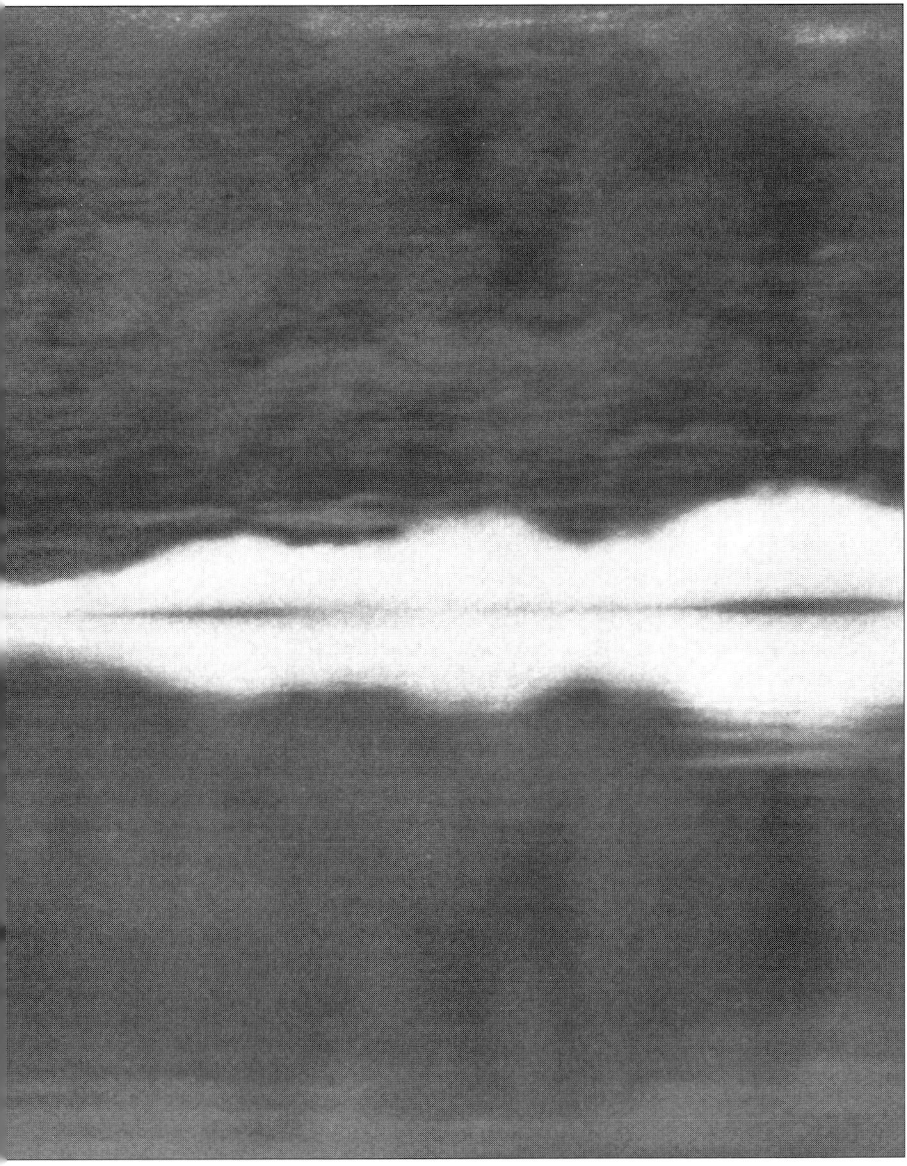

One of the concrete boats now used as a houseboat on the Rhine, near Amsterdam.

The German 'tourists' had clearly done a good job and earmarked areas for bombing, particularly around the Barrow shipyard. The blitz of the town should have been, and indeed was, anticipated and prepared for.

Chapter 2

The Blitz

I can clearly remember Hitler's air force being totally destroyed when I was four years old. I was sitting in an Anderson shelter in May 1941 and listening to our anti-aircraft guns shooting down all the aircraft belonging to the Luftwaffe. This is what my mother told me and I believed her.

What I was really hearing was the sound of bombs falling on the town of Barrow and landing close to the dockland area where we lived. Thankfully, young children accept what they are told and my mother was only shivering with cold despite the fact that it was May!

The bombings of London, Coventry, Manchester and Liverpool were all in the front line and many more civilians were killed in those cities than in Barrow, which got off fairly lightly. But if a bomb lands close to you, it makes no difference whether you are in London, Coventry, Liverpool, Manchester or even in Cologne, Dresden, Munich or Berlin!

On the morning following the night of 7th May 1941 I was taken to see the damage 'caused by German bombers crashing' and found that Barrow's Central Station and my beloved *Coppernob* were buried beneath a heap of smoking rubble. *Coppernob* was a steam locomotive of 1860s vintage which had been on proud display in a huge glass case. For years

Barrow-in-Furness Central passenger station lying in ruins, 7 May 1941.

Coppernob *in its glory days.*

I thought that the old engine had gone for scrap until 2005 when I visited the National Railway Museum in York with my grandson. There, restored to all its glory, was *Coppernob*, so-named because of the shape of its boiler. A plaque pointed out that the engine had been used to move heavy goods around the Barrow docks from 1866 to its retirement and interment in the glass case in 1899. At last I could forgive the Luftwaffe!

The emergency services must have been at full stretch in May 1941, as 87-year-old Betty Kirkland recalls: 'I'll bet you will have collected lots of memories of the blitz in Barrow but I think my experience was unique. I was working in the Timber Corps which was a branch of the Land Army and we were felling trees in the Grizedale Forest. I cut my wrist on a saw and I was driven in a hurry to Barrow hospital. This was the morning following the blitz and every space was occupied by casualties and there were long queues of walking wounded. I went back to Grizedale and was treated there but I still have weak tendons and an impressive scar.'

Many eyewitnesses, including Syd Wilkes, John Oliver, Billy Whiteside and Eric Rigg, told me that you could hear the bombs whistling down prior to the explosion, and the ground shaking. Geoff Cain made the point: 'I think for me the most frightening thing was not the conventional bomb which you could hear coming but the parachute bomb which was a sort of huge, floating landmine. On the night of the main blitz I was doing fire duty in the shipyard from a position on a large crane, which incidentally was built in Germany and assembled by their technicians. The sirens went and soon after, the bombs began to fall. After the whistlings and explosions had stopped I relaxed and suddenly there was an almighty explosion which knocked me off my feet and I was almost blown off the crane. This was caused by a parachute mine which drifted down silently and the delayed fuse kicked in just when you thought that the danger was over. When I struggled down from the crane and returned to base to give in my report the people in

The Barrow bombing, Hindpool Road 9 May 1941. The crane driver must have had a wonderful view over the damaged areas.

Geoff Cain in retirement 2009.

the control room were surprised to see me alive and well. The firefighters at the works and in the town were also hard pressed and were dealing with lots of blazes caused by incendiary bombs, which were full of phosphorus and designed to set off fires. Obviously I can't prove it statistically but I think that everybody worked harder after an air raid because we were determined to get our own back.'

The Germans were out to cause panic and hoped for a decline in the morale of the civilian population. Hence they dropped not only incendiary and parachute mines but also other deadly little weapons. These included the so-called butterfly bombs which rotated like windmills, were brightly coloured and did not explode until they were touched. Posters were put up in schools pointing out the dangers of booby traps. Any child who was killed in this way was recorded as a 'normal' bombing fatality.

There were a few humorous incidents at the time of the Barrow blitz, as Doris Dickenson told me: 'One of my postmen was on fire duty on the flat roof of the office overlooking Cavendish Dock. He was struggling up the stairs with a long clothes prop, with a sweeping brush fastened to the end of it.

This is not washing left out to dry but an unexploded parachute mine!

When I asked him what this was for he told me that it was to fend off the parachute bombs. I had to tell him that these were huge and heavy mines which his improvised brush would be useless against and he would be much better off running as fast as he could.'

Low-level bombing was not an option at any time, let alone at night, and most pilots released their bombs from between 10,000 and 20,000 feet. Any bomb landing on target was a result of pure luck rather than good judgement. Sneak raids by single low-flying aircraft were deterred by the presence of very friendly looking barrage balloons. Albert Marsden remembers how he felt when he saw what looked like flying elephants tethered over the Barrow docks: 'These days we are all used to seeing observation balloons above sporting events like cricket matches, or smaller ones tethered above car showrooms and other retail outlets. I don't think many people realise how huge and comforting these barrage balloons were as they hovered over our towns. One of my aunts worked at the Dunlop rubber factory in Manchester, which made balloons. She had moved from Cleator Moor to get married and found a job at Dunlop's. She told us that the balloons were huge and were accompanied by trailers loaded with gas cylinders. Each balloon was more than 60 feet long and 30 feet high when inflated. Thousands were made and each cost £100 and there was a further £25 for the gas used to inflate the balloon. I remember to this day that she was clean as a new pin but she and lots of the wedding guests smelled of rubber!'

Something else which smelled of rubber was the infamous gas mask which everybody had to carry. Memories were still strong of the First World War trenches festooned in evil green or mustard coloured gas and, as the next conflict loomed, everyone was sure each bombing raid would rain down canisters of deadly chemicals. In the event neither belligerent used the evil stuff but this did not prevent what amounted to gas hysteria from central government downwards. There were lighter moments and a popular rhyme was sung anywhere from

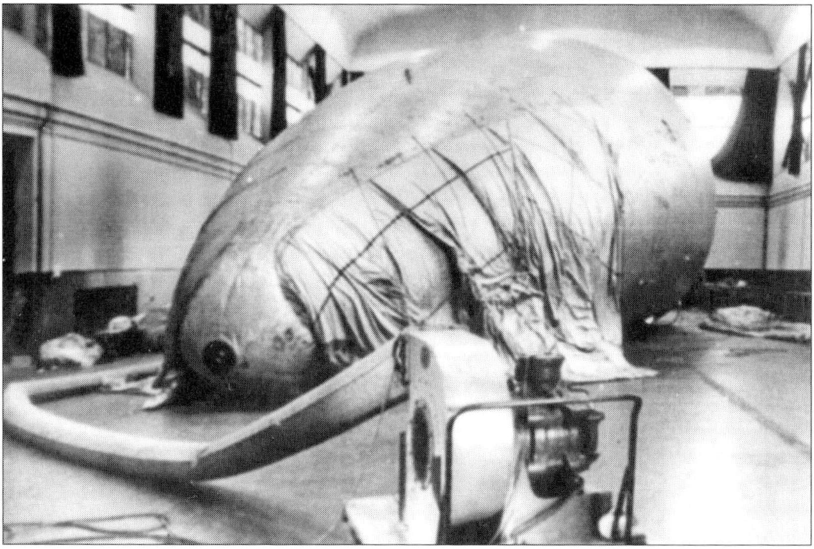

A barrage balloon on test.

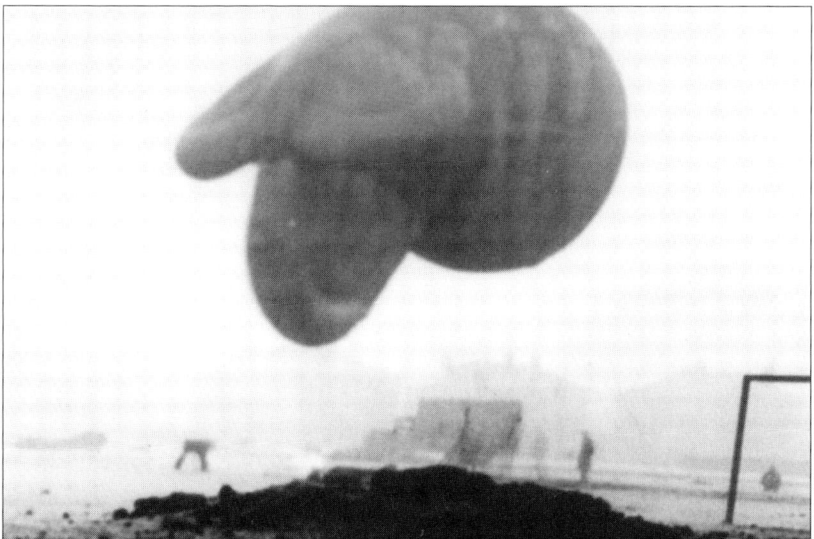

A barrage balloon on duty.

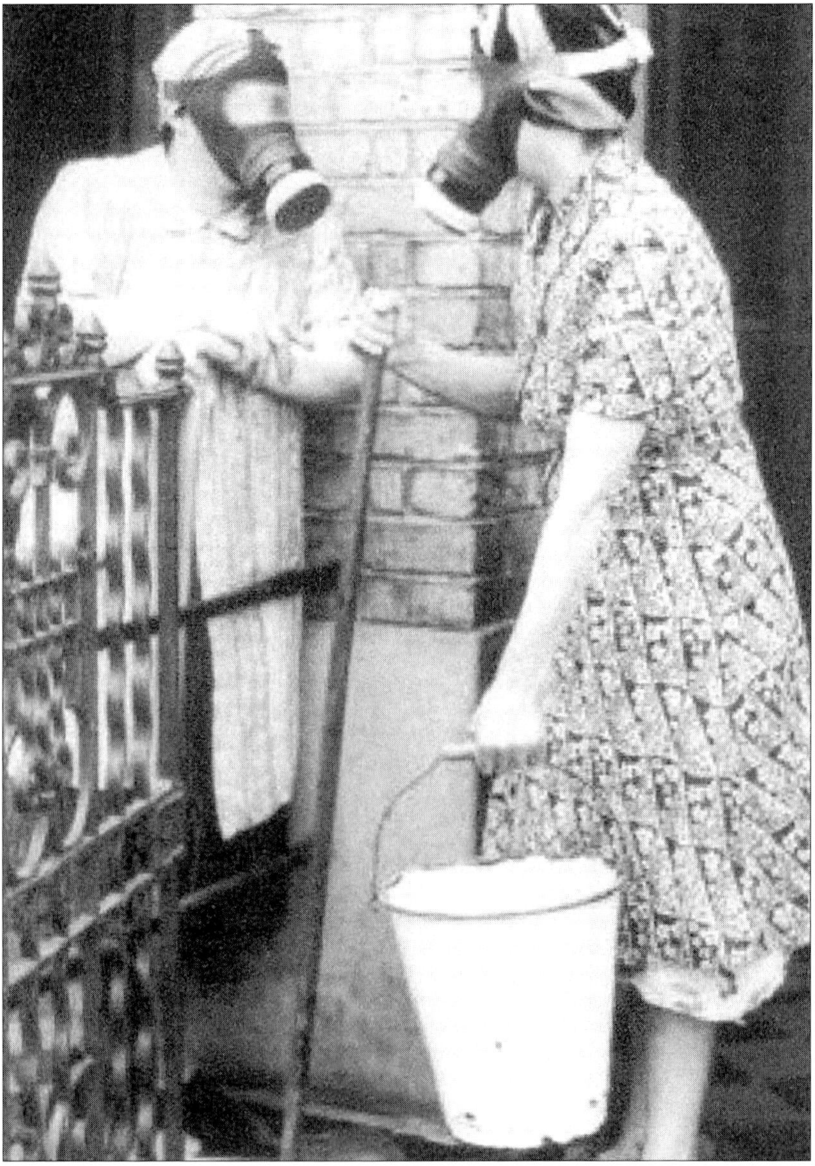

Humour was never far from the surface. 'Over the garden wall' tells its own story, as does the dog with its gas mask.

school playgrounds, church halls and even in factories during meal breaks:

Under the spreading chestnut tree
Neville Chamberlain said to me,
If you want to get your gas mask free
Join the blinking ARP.

Alan Bowes remembers an episode during his schooldays at Appleby-in-Westmorland: 'When the gas masks arrived we were all scared stiff of them. We had to take them to school where we had a special sports day race where all of us wore our gas masks. We all laughed even when the visors steamed up as we got warm.'

There were commercial firms ever eager to jump on the band, or should it be the gas, wagon? Joyce Bradley who was living near Carlisle, remembers her gas mask, those of her family and a few unusual variations: 'The very young 'uns had gas masks that looked like Mickey Mouse which it was hoped stopped them from being frightened of them. We had a posh lady living in a big house near us and my mum used to clean for her. The lady went to Manchester before the war started and bought several gas masks. There was one for the baby and you could put the baby inside and use a handle to pump air in and out of it. This made sense but what made us laugh is that she bought gas masks in which to put her two cats and another for her dog.'

A scout dog – well prepared!

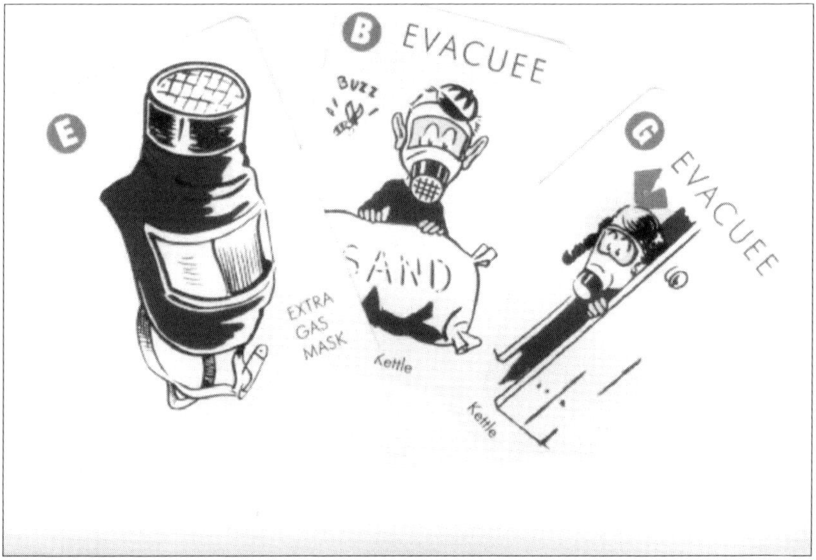

Card games were sold to prevent children being too scared to put their gas masks on.

Doris Porter, who now lives in retirement in Keswick, sent me a cutting dated 23rd October 1939 and pointed out that the Germans must have thought it contained a secret message because who cares about dogs? The newspaper entry read:

> *Many householders are now displaying a card inviting people caught in air-raids whilst exercising their dogs to shelter in their homes. Now it is further suggested that dogs should be equipped with muzzles whilst sheltering. Another suggestion is for a sedative to be given to highly-strung dogs ... The card referred to above can be obtained from the National Canine Defence league, Victoria Station House, London SW1.*

There was a more serious side to a potential gas attack, as Meg Brocklebank remembers: 'At the start of the war we were all

The ARP prepare by testing the efficiency of a gas cape.

An ARP warden holding up a gas cape.

scared stiff that we would be gassed as well as bombed. My grandfather lived with us and as he had been in the first war he was asked if he had seen a gas attack. When he said yes he was immediately identified as a potential expert. He was drafted into the Auxiliary Fire Service and was sent to Manchester to train in gas defence. He spent two hectic weeks dressed up in gas-proof clothing, almost lived in his gas mask and learned to carry a cape which he said made him feel like a bloody bull fighter. He had to take his turn to be a victim and was stripped naked in the decontaminating unit and scrubbed with a huge sweeping brush. He was then sent home and was provided with a lot of equipment which was kept locked in a room marked 'Secret'. Until the day he died he laughed at these preparations which he was convinced would not work but it did keep up morale.'

If gas masks proved not to be needed, the same cannot be said of the air raid shelters. Prominent types were the Anderson, Morrison and so-called community shelters.

Andersons were part and parcel of almost every garden in Cumbria and when I asked for memories of the war in a Radio Cumbria programme, the majority of responses related to air raid shelters. John Bush, now in his eighties and living in Wrexham in North Wales, recalls: 'I suppose I was inspired to find work digging trenches for the laying of electric cables when we lived in Barrow and I helped my dad dig the hole for our Anderson shelter. Dad had been badly wounded in the first war and so had our next-door neighbour. This fella decided that he was not spoiling his garden and in any case he wasn't frightened of Hitler. When the first siren sounded we made our way to the shelter but we were not quick enough. Our neighbour, his wife and three kids were already in there and there was no room for us. On the next morning I excavated his Anderson and got more experience in the digging of 'oles.'

Monica Shackley, who also lived in Barrow, has fonder memories of the family Anderson: 'At first, as children, we were frightened of it and only went into it during air raids. As

An Anderson shelter ready for action.

the news from the war got brighter and we grew older, our Anderson was a play area. My grandad who lived with us had done as he was told and piled up the earth from the hole on top of the shelter and planted it not only with potatoes but also with roses and sweet peas. It was a smashing den and when we were grown up and dad was back from the war he used it for years as his garden shed.'

Elsie Postlethwaite, who lived in Kirkby Lonsdale until she married in 1952, remembers her family's Anderson: 'We furnished it by cutting up an old wardrobe and using the wood for shelves. On these we had lamps, paraffin and airtight tins of Oxo, tea, sugar and dried milk. There was also a small primus stove. Oh ay, and my gran insisted on having the family Bible held over her head once the siren had sounded.'

Margaret Neild, who lived near Broughton, recalls how welcome the Morrison shelter was: 'It arrived and was assembled inside instead of being out in the cold like the Anderson. I was about seven when we got ours. It had a big iron tabletop supported on strong legs which were bolted on. There were then sides made of metal netting which when closed shut off the whole of the shelter. There were four kids in our family and only two bedrooms. The space inside the Morrison was big enough for me and my sister who was five to sleep in and the lads could share the bedroom. The table we had before the Morrison was not big enough for us all to sit round and so for years after the war we used the shelter as our dining room table and it looked posh with a tablecloth on it. My dad went by train early each morning to the Vickers shipyard where he worked as a carpenter and my mum looked after our very large allotment and hen pen. She also kept rabbits which bred, as rabbits are prone to do, and did not count towards our rations. My grandad also kept pigeons from which we made pies. We did not fare too badly and the Morrison table was always full of goodies. As my auntie kept bees the honey was as good as an extra sugar ration.'

Some families, however, were not so well sheltered as Dan

A Morrison shelter was much warmer than the exterior Anderson and doubled up as a table with a bed underneath as shown in this museum exhibit.

Seward recalls: 'I were just old enough to have started work as a labourer in the shipyard and then the bombing started. Some say that it weren't so bad as in Liverpool but that doesn't matter if a bomb hits you! We lived on the top floor of a tenement block close to the docks – too bloody close at times – and we had commercial brick-built shelters in the street. They weren't just brick because they had strengthening wires between the layers. In the shipyard we had better shelters but before going into them we had to be sure that the steam engines and laden wagons were put into stronger places and if it was your turn the fire points had to be manned.'

During the Barrow blitz of May 1941 not everybody trusted the shelters, as Bill Ousby, who was a post office worker in the town, told me: 'Many people ignored the shelters and spent the night in Sowerby Woods. The trail of people was reminiscent of a movement of refugees. Knowing what we now know of how inaccurate the bombing was, the folk were in as much danger of being hit as they would have been in the town shelters. My brother worked in the coalmines at Whitehaven and he felt safe at work but he also told me that many folk took refuge in the cellars of pubs. When I asked him if he enjoyed this he grinned and said that it depended upon how well the publican kept his beer!'

It comes as a surprise to many that the London blitz brought work to the workers in Ulverston, especially the willing women of the town eager to help in the war effort. When the Oxley electronics firm was destroyed by bombing in the capital in 1942, it re-located to the Priory Park area of Ulverston and went on to develop ground-breaking night vision equipment for aircraft.

Although only Barrow was seriously bombed, the German aircraft passed over Cumbria on their way to bomb Glasgow and so the threat was always there, particularly in the coastal areas, until the end of 1943. The danger of an invasion from Southern Ireland being ever present, each time the siren went to warn of aircraft, people waited for the extra sound of church bells being rung to denote that the enemy was landing.

Most people seeking protection from their shelters did not fully appreciate the important job done by the ARP wardens. In 1938 the Home Secretary asked for volunteers to 'assist with Air Raid Precautions'. By 1939 one and a half million people were registered as wardens, 25% of them women. A high-ranking official, often a town clerk, co-ordinated the wardens whose job it was to fill in a report following each period of duty. They could refer to a booklet to explain their duties but they had to pay one penny for this privilege! The wardens were part-time and not paid but provided a much-needed service, especially in periods of bombing.

The portrayal in the TV programme *Dad's Army* of them as 'little Hitlers' and the screaming sound of 'put that light out' did not really give a true picture of the value of the service.

These epithets were not justified, as Marjorie Jinks recalls: 'My father was an ARP warden in Barrow during the war and because of his bulk he was called "Goering" by those he was "spying on". He told me that this was his name on a good day. When he had more problems to cope with he was called "Bloody Gestapo". He laughed at this and the fact that he retained these names long after the war was over. What people did not realise is that Junior Wardens had people over them to ensure that they did the job properly and filled in the report forms correctly. He had great fun and told of the day of the blitz when he had to dig out an old lady. She emerged with just a few bruises and was covered in dust. She was clutching two bags. In one was her rations and in the other she had a huge tom cat screaming to be let out. One of his friends failed to get an Active Service Medal when he was injured. He was carrying a baby to safety when it poked him in the eye with a rattle.'

Audrey Hutton who now lives in Canterbury wrote: 'My father-in-law worked during the war as an ARP warden in, I think, Workington and was later moved to Barrow. He told us that he was given all the training but missed all the action. In 1990 he still had his ARP badge and an axe designed to hack its way into bomb-damaged buildings. He also said that he had visited Preston in the late 1930s and bought a book called *A Practical Guide for the Householder and Air Raid Wardens*. This book is now in my son's collection and I guess that there won't be many of these left. Some of grandad's neighbours and fellow ARP wardens copied out bits of useful information and pinned these up on the wall, which they identified as the safest part of the building. Everybody was a scout in those days and always prepared.'

Once the bombs had fallen, a massive clean-up and rebuilding operation had to be put in force and this meant that workers in factories which made bricks had to work overtime. John Tyson remembers: 'Askam brickworks have always had the advantage of being alongside the main railway line to Barrow and I can't remember how many hours a day my dad

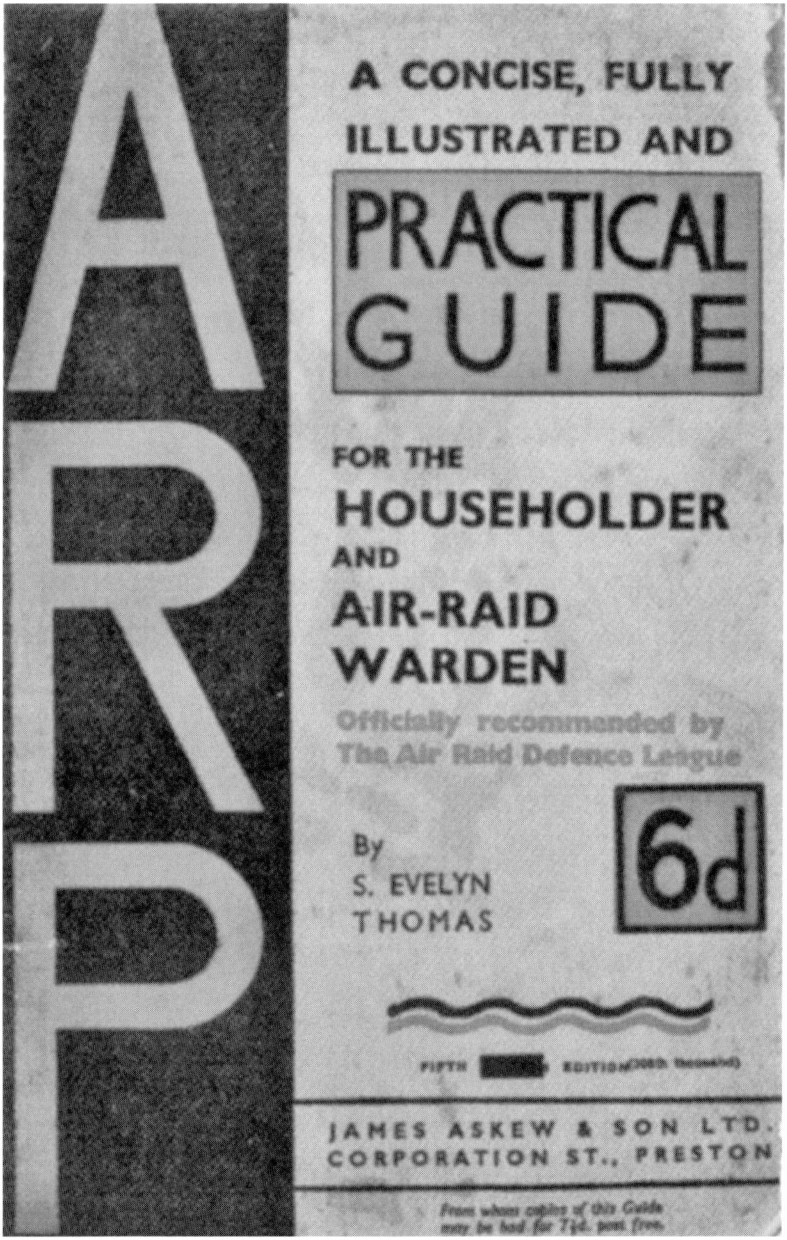
ARP
A CONCISE, FULLY
ILLUSTRATED AND
PRACTICAL
GUIDE
FOR THE
HOUSEHOLDER
AND
AIR-RAID
WARDEN
Officially recommended by
The Air Raid Defence League
6d
By
S. EVELYN
THOMAS
JAMES ASKEW & SON LTD.
CORPORATION ST., PRESTON

worked after the bombing of 1941. We hardly ever saw him and when he came home from the heat of the furnaces he was really dehydrated and drunk water like a thirsty camel. My main memory was that I was given extra pocket money from his wages and I bought some aircraft recognition books which I got thanks to my future brother-in-law who was an ROC observer in Millom.'

Apart from bricks, more slate was needed than ever to repair damage and for new constructions. The slate quarry workers around Kirkby-in-Furness were also hard at work outdoors and in all weathers.

Obviously the wardens were especially busy during air raids but the more warning that could be given the better. It was here that the work of the Royal Observer Corps (the ROC) was so important. It had its origins in the First World War and by 1935 the Corps had extended its range to cover most of Britain. There was a network of members all of whom were skilled in aircraft recognition and their work resulted in King George VI giving the Observer Corps the extra epithet of 'Royal'.

Harry Holmes has fond memories of the ROC: 'I was just a young lad when the war started but I learned to love aeroplanes by listening and learning from older lads and one girl, who was better than any of the bunch. They could identify most aircraft in the world, not only on the ground but more importantly in the air. They bought books to help them and I remember one being called *Silhouettes in the Sky – A Scientific Height Finder*.'

Some of these lads joined the Royal Observer Corps and went to work all over the north-west of England, including posts around the Cumbrian coast. Look-out posts were carefully selected and included disused lighthouses. There was one on the coast at Millom and all they did was fence it round the top with a railing and use part of the inside as a mess and rest area. There was another at Maryport on the site of what had been a Roman signal station. Later on they learned to use sophisticated height-finding equipment, but they had the obvious disadvantage of not being able to see at night but some

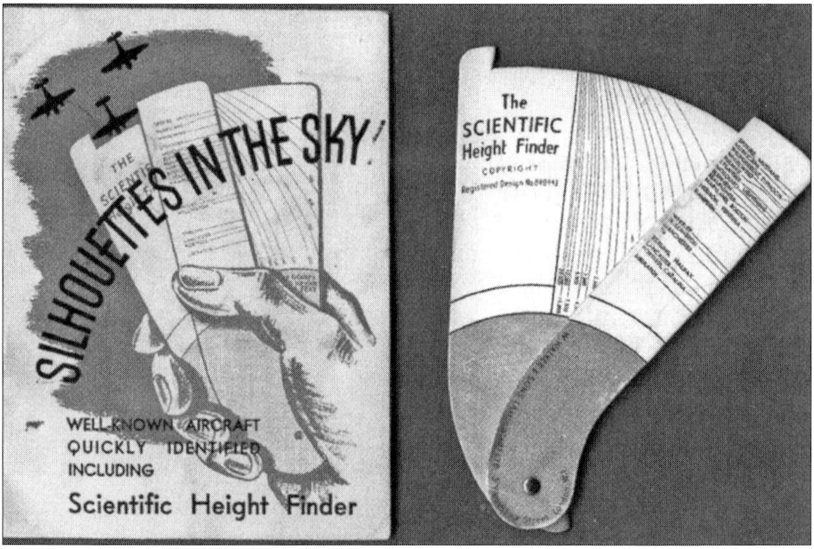

became very skilled at identifying the various types by the sound of the engine. Even when radar came into play the ROC was still regarded as vital.

Alan Yates also remembers the skilful work of members of the ROC: 'I have always been interested in the bases of the Corps during the war. I found the Millom station which you mentioned and there were others, obviously around Barrow but also at St Bees, Whitehaven and Workington, in addition to the Roman station you mentioned at Maryport, but there they also used the lighthouse. I think that there was one at the top of the Hoad monument in Ulverston. Even when the observers knew that the bombers were going to fly over them they had excellent telephone links with Glasgow and so gave them advanced warning.'

The work of the ROC was important not only as a warning signal for towns but also to those controlling the movement of traffic on major roads and especially along vulnerable railway routes. Most rail traffic in the war involved troop movements or armaments and the general public was asked not to travel.

The Royal Observer Corps' site at Millom in the 1940s. Old lighthouses were easily adapted.

There were notices everywhere asking people, 'Is your journey really necessary?'.

Railway workers were under constant pressure as engine driver Billy Barnes remembered all too well: 'The war were difficult but exciting and I usually operated my locomotive between Carnforth and Carlisle but, when the pressure were on, me and my fireman went as far as Crewe and occasionally to London. During the build-up to Normandy we went to the invasion ports. We often had to crew old and often very dirty engines and they took time to fire up in the mornings. Sometimes the repair workers were still at it when we were set to leave. There was no time to clean either the engine or the rolling stock and at times the passenger carriages were so mucky that you could not see through the windows. In our case the muck from the engine was smothered by the coating of engine oil and coal dust.

'Both me and my fireman loved the open air of the cab. In the war things were difficult and we had a real problem. The firebox had to be kept away from the "eyes in the sky" and the footplate area was covered all over by a thick light-proof tarpaulin sheet. In that area we felt that we were being boiled alive. We were also told in no uncertain terms that we must not disclose either our destination or details of our corps even after we got home. Most times we did not know where we were going until we reported for duty and if the load was sensitive we did not know until we were finally coupled up. In 1944 I had to take a train load full of Yanks to Southampton and a mate of mine took some more troops to Portsmouth. We were buggered when we got home but not so buggered as them poor lads on their way to the beaches of Normandy.

'Sometimes, if we changed shifts at Carnforth, we could go into the rest room and enjoy a cup of tea and a sandwich provided by the WVS ladies who often kept the kettle boiling all through the day and night. I still get a thrill when my grandkids take me to the Railway Museum at York and I can see the wartime locomotives all looking spruced up. There is a big engine called *Dame Vera Lynn*. I often wonder what the old lady herself would look like covered in muck.'

Tom Brewer has made a study of the railways at war and he made a valid point: 'You must remember that, at the start of the war, there were a lot more lines than there are today and four main companies were operating. The government took over the running of the railways and if they had not developed a co-ordinated system there would have been chaos.'

It was not just the crews on the railways that were kept on their toes during the war. A friend of my wife's father was Bill Donley, who worked as a signalman on the Settle to Carlisle line. Bill recalled: 'I remember the stretch at Dent during the winters of 1941 and 1942 when the snow was so deep that I was stranded in my box but I did have a coke fire to keep warm and to brew up on. I felt sorry for the soldiers who were drafted in to shift the snow from the line. The Settle to Carlisle was the only link (and still is) between the East and West coast routes between Scotland and London. If either of the main lines were closed, then traffic could be diverted along our link. We were run off our feet in the lead up to the Normandy landings as troops, mostly Americans who had been training in Cumbria and Scotland, were ferried down to the embarkation ports.

'I was one of the lucky ones because all I had to do was sit in my box. I could feel the warmth of the sun in the summer and in winter listen to the sleet, rain and wind. I felt sorry for the maintenance crews who had to check the track even when a force ten wind was blowing. This is still one of the remotest and windiest spots in Britain and some of those lads on the line must have needed lead in their boots. I loved it when I could have a crack with the farmers who were on their way to markets at Settle on the down line or Appleby on the up stretch. Every so often I was tossed a rasher of streaky bacon or a couple of eggs packed safe in a box of straw. I was as nimble a fielder as any cricketer! I cooked these goodies on a shovel which I stuck into the fire hole of my stove. On a few occasions I paid for a rabbit to take home. These were caught by local lads, who set traps on land adjacent to the track.

'Obviously I was aware that there was a war on because I had to sign what was I suppose the Official Secrets Act to say that I would not divulge any details of the cargoes carried along the line. I saw tanks, shells, aeroplane parts and rations such as tea and sugar. There was even a truck loaded with Lucky Strike fags, which I guess were the supplies for the Yanks. My job was essential but not dangerous and I was working in the heart of the most beautiful area in England. I did have to make sure that as daylight faded the signal box did not contravene blackout regulations.'

Throughout the war, but especially in the early 1940s after which the threat of bombs falling in Cumbria diminished, the blackout precautions were strictly enforced and moving about at night was a real problem. As mentioned above, enforcing these regulations was one, but only one, of the duties of the ARP wardens, but the Home Guard always kept a wary eye open for offenders. In some places there was a large model clock with its hands indicating the lighting up times. Kerbs and the bases of tree trunks were painted white, cars and bikes had screens on their lights and indicators and people were asked to use bulbs of minimal wattage.

Jonah Walker drove buses for the Ribble Company during the war and these operated all over Cumbria. He told me: 'We had big red double-decker Leylands and we knew that war were coming when the passenger windows were fitted with blinds and criss-crossed with tape to prevent glass from flying about. The bumpers and fenders were painted white and the headlights dimmed so that we could hardly see at night.'

Jonah was known to be a fast driver and he felt aggrieved when his timetable was disrupted: 'It were bad enough having to drive slowly but even worse was when we were continually stopped by the Home Guard who inspected the identity card of each passenger and even mine and my clippie's were looked at. This stop and search occurred all over Cumbria especially

The police on night duty in 1941.

where German and Italian POW camps were nearby. Another thing which slowed us up was what we called "tank blocks". These were huge concrete slabs arranged so that the traffic had to weave around them. It certainly worked because it reduced traffic to a crawl. One thing, which we did not expect but we soon learned to look out for, was spivs who learned to siphon off the fuel at the terminus if we left the vehicle to have a break. I'm a big fella and I caught one little runt at my tank. I got hold of him, poured the fuel over him and one of my mates took him to the police station keeping him still by holding a cigarette lighter close to him. I'm glad that he were put away for six months and his name were published in the paper.'

In the event of an invasion, plans were in hand to requisition all private cars and as there were so few on the roads in the 1930s the local police knew who owned vehicles. Some idea of how few cars there were in Cumbria can be seen from

Kirkby Lonsdale in 1935.

postcards and photographs produced in the 1930s. The square at Kirkby Lonsdale, for instance, (see above) has not changed much since the war except that now parking a car at peak periods can often be very difficult.

Despite the strict blackout precautions accidents on the roads and even at home did increase. With regard to traffic, the already hard-pressed police had to do more traffic duty and were sensibly provided with white coats, armbands and gloves so that they could be seen at night.

Shopkeepers had a real problem as doors were continually being opened and closed by customers. Sisters Dora Myerscough and Annie Ellison were working in the Dalton branch of the Maypole grocers during the war. Annie remembers the problems faced in those days: 'During the blackout the store had special thick wooden shutters fitted and we had two doors both with blackout curtains. Customers had to close the first door before opening the second. Travelling by bus or train was also a problem because it was often too dark to see the step, especially for elderly people.'

Brian Lees told me of one incident as he was waiting to alight from a train in the blacked-out Carlisle station. There was a young soldier who was very, very drunk. He did not realise that the train had stopped short of the platform. The soldier opened the door and stepped out onto the lines. He scrambled back into the carriage, adjusted his cap and opened the opposite door. Down he went onto the track for the second time and soon emerged back into the carriage. He must have been so drunk that he did not hurt himself and once the train reached the platform he tottered off into the night!

What has emerged most clearly as I wrote this chapter is that the war in Cumbria was fought partly in the factories and in keeping the transport system running, but also partly by the humour of the folk who echoed Winston Churchill's optimism and never thought that they could lose. Churchill said, 'Let us go forward together', and they did!

Chapter 3

War at Sea and in the Air

When he heard that I was going to compile a book on Cumbria at war, a historian friend of mine who lives and works in Essex exclaimed, 'Surely nothing happened there of any real significance?' I pointed out to him that there were lots of industries in the three counties which now make up Cumbria and that vital war work went on to provide munitions for the army, navy and air force. All this was best done away from the more vulnerable areas closest to occupied Europe. The Germans knew this and their espionage activities have been described in chapter one. Ships also had to be built in a hurry, and pilots and aircrews trained as far away as possible from the main areas of conflict.

The north-west of England was ideally suited for these vital activities and consequentially the Vickers Armstrong shipyard would certainly have been a prime target for the Germans and the workers there fully realised that they might well be in the firing line.

Those who think that the skies over what is now Cumbria were peaceful during the war need to think again. A paper dated November 1939 written by Major Joseph Schmidt, who was the Head of Luftwaffe Intelligence, states:

> *The most important ports must be attacked without exception and as far as possible simultaneously. The intermixture of residential areas with dockyards in some British ports is no reason not to attack such ports. The most important ports are those of London, Liverpool, Hull, Bristol and Glasgow.*

Barrow too was obviously an important target and Cumbria was on the flight path to Glasgow. There are recorded eyewitness reports of aerial dog fights over Cumbria and these are backed up by the pilots' reports from fighter stations based at Squires Gate, Blackpool and Woodvale near Southport.

I had several long and informative meetings with Glynn Griffiths at the RAF Millom Museum. He told me: 'We have lots of combat reports and photographs relating to Woodvale and Squires Gate, with their Spitfires doing battle with German Dorniers. The enemy knew the value of these fighter squadrons and they had detailed photographs of the airfields. They failed to hit either of them and the "Spits" may well have diverted attacks on the smaller ports such as Maryport, Millom, Whitehaven and Workington. The Luftwaffe directive was to use just a few aircraft to attack these ports with the intention of destroying fuel dumps, harbour installations, ships and ration stores.'

Shipbuilding in Barrow was very much a family affair and most fathers working in the yard would make sure that their sons carried on the trade and hoped that the next generation would continue the tradition.

1942: A Luftwaffe bombing plan to attack Woodvale (which they called Formby). If this was damaged, then the German bombers would have a clear run to Barrow, the Cumbrian ports and Glasgow.

Woodvale 1942: The presence of the main road meant that the airfield was difficult to camouflage but, as this photograph indicates, some attempts were made to bomb the facility. (Millom RAF Museum)

Geoff Cain takes up the story: 'Whilst to a few men the shipyard was just a job, this was the exception and the majority took a real pride in the surface ships and submarines which they helped to build. Most followed the career of each vessel and even during the war when paper shortages reduced the number of pages in the *North Western Evening Mail* they scanned the print to find news both good and bad of vessels built in Barrow. It wasn't just the local lads who worked in the yard. There were what were known as the workmen's trains which brought men in their hundreds from far flung places all over Cumbria. This was a regional workforce and one which the present residents of Cumbria should be proud of.'

I have personal connections with the yard as in the early years of the war we lived alongside the small station which was the terminus for the workmen's trains. I still remember well the shift changes as one workmen's trainload alighted to be

The Officers' Mess at RAF Millom is now a museum.

replaced by those ending their shift and on their way home. If I close my eyes I can still hear the hiss of steam, the sound of the engine's whistle and the clip-clap of clogs beating out a rhythm on the pavements.

I also had four uncles who were born-and-bred shipyard men. My three maternal uncles were all in the Shipyard Brass Band, which was famous and won many contests all over the north-west of England and also at London's Albert Hall. On launch days the bands were impressive in their pristine uniforms and their instruments shone brightly even on the dullest of days.

It was not just the warships which played a vital role in the war, although in the context of this book they will receive the most attention. The ocean liners discarded their paying passengers and also went to war, as I found out when I spoke to Graham Cubbin: 'Here in the Dock Museum we have impressive models of the liner *Orama* built in 1924 and the *Orion* constructed during the early 1930s. The *Orama* was sunk by the German vessel *Admiral Hipper* whilst evacuating troops from Narvic in Norway in 1940. The *Orion* fared much better and was painted in battleship grey and converted to a troop carrier. She was a vital part of the North African landings in 1943 and after the war was over she ferried troops from Europe to their native Australia and New Zealand before being taken out of service in 1946.'

Stan Hughes, who was born in Ulverston and whose father worked in the shipyard, has fond memories of the *Orion*: 'I joined my regiment on the way to North Africa and boarding the troop ship realised that it was the Barrow liner. My dad was a carpenter and so I touched the woodwork to give me luck. It must have worked because I'm nearly 90 and still going strong.'

There was one Barrow-built vessel which, thankfully, was not so lucky! She was a battle cruiser called the *Congo* and she was bought for the Japanese Navy. She was torpedoed in the Pacific in 1944 by the American submarine *Sealion*, with the loss of more than 1,000 Japanese lives.

There was other important work going on in the yard apart from building ships and Jimmy Weatherburn has vivid memories of these events: 'There was a lot of work to do repairing vessels damaged by enemy action. It soon became obvious that only a very special sort of chap could do the initial work which involved assessing the damage. They had to scramble among the wreckage and they nearly always found bits of bodies, or complete but mangled and often stinking corpses. I heard one of these chaps say that he had just been sick but he was now ready to write his damage report after handing in the dead sailors' identity tags. He then went on to say that we all owed it to these sad victims to get the ship ready for sea and ensure that the very bloody war was won. None of us at the time had room to grieve for the German sailors. To us each and every one of 'em was a Hitler. Now that time has softened the hurt, we can sympathise with the other side but still be happy that we won.'

The Orama, *sunk by the Germans in 1940.*

The Orion, *survived the war and took part in the North African landings in 1943.*

The shipyard did not just involve itself with the shell of the vessel and its fixtures and fittings. Something very powerful has to drive the ships through the water. Geoff Cain, now well into his eighties, reminded me of this as I drank tea in his neat sitting room with magnificent views of the Cumbrian countryside.

'I worked all my life on marine engines and these were huge, heavy and very complex. They had to be engineered to precise tolerances and follow detailed drawings. This work always fascinated me and no engineer whose work means the safety of thousands of men can afford to be slipshod. A broken-down engine or propeller gearing is just as crippling as an enemy torpedo. Look at any engineer and you will see a tidy chap – those who were not tidy got sacked. I worked on the engines of many warships, including the aircraft carrier *Illustrious*, and also some of the luxurious liners. Warships had to be functional and with regard to engines they were not part of an ocean liner's luxury. All the power plant had to do was to keep working. My job was to formulate drawings for electrical circuits and I became head of such an office. I changed an overall for a posh suit, but as in any successful company, it was all down to team work.'

I'm also glad that I have kept a diary since I was in my teens. I will never forget my uncle, Wilf Ellison, who lived on High Cleator Street in Dalton-in-Furness. He was a Rolls-Royce trained fitter and turner and in the war he worked in the Vickers shipyard. In 1981 he told me, 'Many folk think that all that Vickers did in the war was build ships but actually we did a lot more than that. I worked on big guns and we had to rifle the gun barrels to a very precise tolerance. We knew that if we got it wrong the gun would not function properly. With my Rolls-Royce training I was aware that folk who got it wrong quickly got the sack. The concept of not wasting anything was very much in our minds and all the metal turnings were collected and melted down to make new weapons.'

Another of my uncles was Billy Whiteside, who operated a

crane: 'We were either run off our feet or had nowt to do. There were times in winter when it was wet and windy and we were freezing cold and even climbing up and down was hard, especially when the air raid siren sounded. Once we realised that there would probably be no more bombing we could enjoy the spectacular views over the busy docks where submarines and surface ships were taking shape.'

Dan Archer made another interesting point about working in the yard: 'Shipbuilding involved all sorts of different trades. There were people in the foundries, there were moulders pouring hot metal, and fitters and turners who fine-tuned the engines. There were boiler and engine makers, skilled carpenters, electricians and plumbers who fitted out the shells of ships after they had been launched. Each of the trades obviously operated in their own shops, which were like little villages that together made up a town full of different skills. Then there were the lads who were there when the ships were put to sea to carry out trials.'

Stan Howells was at pains to point out: 'One thing which is seldom mentioned is that in the mid-1930s British industry was in recession and there was no capital to invest in new machinery. We spent almost as much time repairing antiquated machinery as we did in operating it. In contrast the German priorities were to prepare for war and they had new and more efficient machines. This is why they wanted Norway because iron ore could be imported through the Nordic routes. We all knew that we had a real challenge on our hands and we literally had to swim and not sink.'

Raymond Mullen continued in this theme: 'I was an electrician in the yard and we all knew the value of raw materials, such as rubber and copper. Things were not going at all well in the early days when we were working at full speed and fast running out of raw materials that were mainly sourced from overseas. This put even more pressure on the merchant fleet, but we had a bonus when the bulk of the Norwegian fleet fled en masse to Britain. These lads braved the perils normally associated with the sea but also had to run the gauntlet of the German navy, especially the U-boats. There were lots of shortages and we always made the merchant navy lads welcome when they docked and brought us essential supplies. You should go and talk to George Hutchinson and he will tell you how good quality timber was so valued during the war.'

I found 88-year-old George living in Millom and he vividly remembered this time: 'I used to travel to Vickers in what we called the workmen's train. I were a ship's carpenter and even before the war started we were told not to waste even one inch of timber. Much of this came from Scandinavia and came through the Norwegian ports and when these were overrun by the Germans the timber had to come from somewhere else and involved the perilous crossing of the Atlantic. We got some ladders from converted cotton bobbin mills including one at Stott Park near Newby Bridge but this was just a drop in the ocean. The hard timber had to come from Canada. Not only did we have to conserve timber but we were told not to waste nails, screws, bolts, washers and hinges. When we were repairing vessels damaged in action, we had to recycle as many materials as possible, especially the woodwork of the decking. We did not need our wives to tell us to "make do and mend" during the war. Britain had imported trees for centuries and lots of trees were cut down during the first war. Everybody knows that it takes upwards of 60 years to grow a useable tree from a sapling. Aye – it's true! Every tradesman knew that it was a sin to waste owt.'

I travelled to meet George by train and as I returned from Millom to Barrow I realised that I was following the same route as the wartime 'workmen's train', passing through Greenroad, Foxfield, Kirkby and Askam. I then went on to Ulverston where at one time there was a link to Lakeside on Windermere and which is still the berth for the pleasure steamers. Part of the line from Haverthwaite to Lakeside is a steam-hauled track once again which is popular with tourists. Even the pleasure steamers were commandeered during the war so it was now not just a case of war at sea but also 'war at lake', as Sam Winstanley recalls:

'Before the war started I used to look forward to a day out with my parents. We travelled by train from Ulverston to Lakeside and then onto the steamers for a circular trip around Windermere. I remember eating Smith's crisps which had a blue paper twist inside containing salt and I also drank a bottle of Thompson's fizzy dandelion and burdock. As war became imminent these pleasure trips were obviously curtailed. Vessels were taken over and the *Tern* was converted into a training ship for the Navy and was renamed TS (Training Ship) *Ondine*. The *Tern* is still in operation and I now follow the steam train with a tour of the lake, but it is my turn to pay because I am joined by three grandchildren. Apart from the Victorian vintage *Tern* there are the larger vessels called the *Teal* and *Swan*. One of my grandfathers worked on the construction of these recently refurbished craft which were built in Barrow in the 1930s.'

A brew of wartime tea aboard TS Ondine.

Moira Bancroft, who now lives in retirement in Brisbane, recalls her life as a teacher in Cumbria before marrying an Australian airman: 'When you asked me for my memories of the war it set me thinking of the time in Barrow very close to the Vickers Armstrong shipyard. I did not need an alarm clock to get me up in the morning. Just before eight I heard two sounds which still echo in my memory. These were the rhythmic clatter of the clogs on the street or the rattle of the bicycles over the rough roads. Then came the whistle to end one shift and start another. Then came the whistles and hissing of the steam engines which moved goods around the work sheds. There were evenings when I was entertained free of charge by the shipyard band rehearsing. During the war the launch of a vessel was deliberately kept low key but many of the children I taught had fathers who took pride each time a vessel was released off the stocks and hit the water with a huge splash. The school always turned out to watch the ship built to batter Hitler and to wave Union Jacks.

'Nearby was a scrapyard that crushed anything made of iron, which was sent off to be melted down and reconstructed. The crusher consisted of a crane-like structure with a huge iron ball hanging from it. This was then dropped from a great height onto the metal item to be scrapped which was usually an old vehicle. This equipment was known affectionately to the children as "The Big Bonker" and this to me still has a pleasant ring to it, although even at 90 I know that it has a much ruder meaning to it these days! I obviously remember the freezing cold winters of 1940 and 1941 when there was a shortage of coal and the children were often kept at school to keep warm so that parents could conserve fuel. Plans were in hand to evacuate us but in the end we stayed put and, as the bombing threat eased, the children could be taught in safety. All the classrooms had their walls covered in war posters and the children drew bombs, ships, aircraft and, of course, "The Big Bonker".'

The Tern, *adapted from a pleasure steamer to a war training ship called the TS* Ondine.

In the Air

It is not often realised that the area which is now Cumbria had a major part to play in the War in the Air. Apart from the already mentioned Vickers Armstrong shipyard, the huge aircraft enterprise was actually at the forefront of British and aviation history. This I discovered when I spoke to Glynn Griffiths, the curator of the Millom Air Museum, actually housed in the officers' quarters of what was a very large airbase. This is situated at Haverigg on the outskirts of Millom. The main section of the camp is now fenced off and is a prison. Television viewers will know it as Slade Prison, which featured in the Ronnie Barker series *Porridge*.

Glynn Griffiths, however, was able to take me back much further into the history of flying in Cumbria: 'From the early 1890s until the middle of the First World War, Barrow built airships for both military and civilian customers. Around 1912 one of the design team was none other than the famous Barnes Wallis. He became prominent by using lightweight alloys as the framework for the airships. I'm always reminded of Meccano whenever I see these airship designs. There were increased orders as the First World War loomed because the powers that be envisaged war in the air only involved observation "vessels" to locate troop movements. At this time aeroplanes were only regarded as rich men's toys.

'With this viewpoint in mind, Vickers decided to expand the airship business and began to build a huge base near Cark. The idea was to follow the Barrow example and provide accommodation for the workers. The suburb built on Walney Island at Barrow is still known as Vickerstown. As events turned out, aeroplanes soon proved to be more versatile and the airship project had already cost millions of pounds even in those days. Barnes Wallis was moved from his house in Grange-over-Sands and his design skills were adapted to design and build the Wellington bomber which did sterling service, especially during the early years of the conflict. He obviously used his experience to design the lightweight but very strong

The Electronics office at Vickers, with Geoff Cain on the left of the picture.

Wellington aircraft. I feel sorry for Barnes Wallis. His bouncing bombs, which were used only once in the Dam Busters raid on the Ruhr, overshadow his most important role as first an airship and then an aircraft designer of very great talent.'

Glynn then went on to show me another area of the museum which is devoted to mapping out the positions of aircraft which crashed in the north-west of England. I noticed that there were some records of wrecked Avro Anson aircraft. Most people, including aviation historians who should know better, write off Ansons as antiquated old crates designed specifically to crash. I should not be too smug because I also at one time had a low opinion of Ansons. That was until I spoke to the Avro historian Harry Holmes.

Harry first glared at me and then he smiled and his features softened: 'I feel sad and angry when folk malign the Anson. It was designed in the 1930s and was one of Avro's most successful aircraft. Over 11,000 were built in factories all around Manchester. It was designed in peacetime as an up-market passenger aircraft and then as war loomed it was converted into a lightweight bomber. It was only meant as a stop-gap until larger and more powerful bombers came off the production lines. Then the Ansons were moved to Coastal Command and went on the hunt for U-boats. In fact it was an Anson which bombed a U-boat on the surface and sank it. This was the first U-boat to be destroyed in the war. The reason why so many Ansons crashed in what is now Cumbria during the war was due to two factors. Firstly they were based at places like Walney, Cark and Millom and were used for training aircrew, many of whom were Polish or other Eastern Europeans who could speak very little English, although they could use swear words! Many of these became excellent and brave pilots but they were often impetuous and inclined to cut corners, which is always dangerous. Secondly, they also had to learn how to fly low over mountains and I have no doubt that there are still bits of Anson wreckage awaiting discovery.'

Actually the number of crashes declined as the war reached its peak but by 1941 the air stations at Cark and Millom had cooperated to develop a Mountain Rescue Service. In this they were assisted by many locals who knew the terrain well. There was also a good working relationship between air force and army units. Occasionally the rescue groups were helped by volunteers who could speak East European languages and of course doctors were also on hand.

My father told me of his connection with the Polish trainees. Dad was based for a while at Millom and was an expert in radio communications and Morse. His personal cipher machine is on display at the Millom museum. One of his jobs was to guide the pilots home if they got into difficulty with the notoriously sudden and bad visibility typical of the Cumbrian mountains. He was always reluctant to speak about those times when he was still trying to make sense of Anglo-Polish when communications suddenly ceased as the aircraft crashed.

One of my father's friends was an airman called Ralph Watson, known as 'Chorter' for some reason unknown to me. He told me just before he died in Uxbridge in Middlesex: 'I was an aircraft mechanic and I loved working on Ansons. The Anson was beautifully designed and although I had huge hands I could easily get my fingers into all areas of the machine. In wartime the poor old Ansons were worked to death and the young pilots did not always learn to treat them right.'

This aspect of Cumbria at war has very largely been ignored by military historians who deal with the Battle of Britain, the Bombers' War and airfields in and close to south-eastern England. These brave airmen did not just arrive at battle

Electronic communications equipment used by the author's father in 1941. (Millom Air Museum)

Sunderland flying boats were constructed in great secrecy at Whitecross Bay on the banks of Windermere.

stations already trained but were put through the rigours of training and made most of their mistakes around airfields further away from areas of combat.

The public of Cumbria welcomed the aircrews and went to work in armament factories. Whilst some suffered bombing, all were aware of other aspects of war.

Travelling for pure enjoyment was hardly, if at all, possible in the war with petrol rations rigorously applied. We should remember, however, that people were generally more physically active at a time when only the affluent could afford cars. People always walked if possible or else used their bicycles. Joyce Postlethwaite, now well into her eighties, still hops on her bike to the shops but as she put it: 'These are only three miles away. I remember two factories springing up like autumn mushrooms. These were around Whitecross Bay on Windermere. There was a prominent one for processing perch from the lake. These were called Percines or specially selected Lakeland Perch preserved in tomato sauce and what they politely called Yorkshire relish. Why Yorkshire, I have often wondered? They were like sub-standard pilchards but the taste was no doubt masked by the Yorkshire relish. The other not so prominent building, which looked like an extension of the fish processing plant, was used by Short brothers who were producing flying boats. Whenever they were testing one of these there were always lots of soldiers and Home Guard lads on standby and some were on the lake itself in speed boats with guns mounted on them.'

What was even less obvious was that a small part of the Short complex was being used by George Patterson. This man was a very accomplished inventor and he designed and built what is now known as the Patterson glider. These were used to deliver secret agents into German-occupied Europe and especially into Norway. Long after the war, Patterson established a steamboat museum at Bowness-on-Windermere and anyone interested in old restored steamboats cannot afford to miss this excellent attraction. One area is devoted to

The Patterson glider was trialled at Whitecross and was used to deliver secret agents into German occupied territory, especially in Norway.

Patterson's ground-breaking war work and the glider he perfected.

There has been a view that Cumbria played no part in aircraft construction and yet many firms were employed all over the county producing thousands of components. Short Brothers, as Joyce said, were building flying boats in great secret on the banks of Windermere. The U-boat crews knew and feared these Sunderlands and called them 'Flying Porcupines' because of the guns that seemed to sprout all around the fuselage.

With so many vital industries working at full capacity it was obvious to all that these facilities had to be protected not just from a full scale invasion, but also from sabotage and from the eyes of spies.

Chapter 4

The Home Front

During the war people were more friendly with their neighbours and they would talk more easily to strangers on buses and trains, at places of entertainment, in factories and in shops. They would queue without complaining and some did extra, vital jobs even though they were only paid for one of them. There was a feeling that everyone was in it together. As time goes by and people gradually ascend to a more peaceful place the splendid work done by bodies such as the Home Guard, the Women's Voluntary Service (WVS), those who organised the welfare of evacuees and displaced persons as well as churches of all denominations, the YMCA and the always energetic Salvation Army, fade into history.

Children are only young once and they got on with enjoying life and left the adults to do the worrying. Children, especially but by no means exclusively boys, have played war games since the world began. During the war there was a much better substitute than 'Cowboys and Indians'. The baddies were always easy to identify and I have known of fights to determine which poor kids had to be the Germans and learn to play dead! As the conflict began to swing more towards the Allies some of the intense pressure was off and the once strictly enforced no-go areas were gradually relaxed and opened up. My great childhood friend was George Hughes and we had fun around the Furness area of what was then Lancashire. We lived in Furnace Place in an area of Askam still known as the 'Lots'. This was linked to the main village by the Furnace area, the ruined remains of an iron and steel works, which had closed long before the war and was a popular play area. This is now a housing estate. There was the slag bank, known as the Pier, which jutted out into the sea towards Millom. This had been created as the molten slag from the ironworks was poured into the sea, steaming and hissing as it cooled. It was starting to grass over as the war began and is now an unofficial, but very rich and attractive nature reserve.

Close to the slag bank was the 'airman's hut', which was a square building linked to radio systems. This overlooked the sandy beach covered twice each day by the tides on which was sited a target used by trainee aircrew dropping bombs from their Ansons based at the Millom airfield. There was a radio link to the airfield and the accuracy or otherwise of the bombing run was communicated. Some of the airmen were friendlier than others and one of them knew my father. I remember to this day the huge bacon sandwich we had and the packet of bacon I was given to take home to my mother. To me this was the real rigour of war!

After 1945 the hut was abandoned and the shutters and door were left open. What a splendid den this made and although the expensive apparatus had been taken away and the power supply cut off there remained two armchairs, a table and masses of wires and colourful knobs to stimulate the imagination. The place was a miracle to us when it rained.

In 1944 another miracle had happened. The Yanks came and set up a training camp with lots of tents in our Furnace playground. Typical of the Americans, we kids were given candy, cake, comics, rations and empty cigarette packets of types we had never seen before including Lucky Strike. The Americans were certainly a lucky, if temporary, strike for us kids. When they left to go to a serious war we took over their holes, found driftwood from the shore and brewed up stews from carrots, onions, potatoes and cabbages, which we got from our family allotments, then a vital part of every household. This happy episode came to an abrupt halt when we found a cache of live bullets that the troops had left behind as they were summoned in a hurry to Normandy. The local police, in the ample form of Sergeant Skitt and the Scottish P.C. Kirkwood, who looked remarkably like the officer in the *'Allo 'Allo!* television series, conducted a thorough search for more bullets. I now think our two bobbies took their time as it diverted their attention from the unpleasant task of looking for illegal eggs, sugar, cheese and lumps of meat on the black market.

When I left the local school to attend Ulverston Grammar School in 1947 I found classmates who were playing at nights and at weekends in military installations in other parts of the Lake District, especially in pillboxes. My friend Peter Burns and I went on our bikes to Haverthwaite and had our sandwiches in a pillbox guarding the road to Grizedale. We had heard rumours that there had been Nazis nearby during the war but it was only much later that we discovered that the most important POW camp in England was at Grizedale (see chapter seven).

I asked Betty Kirkland if she could remember this particular box: 'Oh yes, I can remember this one and lots of others. When I worked in the Timber Corps at Grizedale one of our jobs was to be taken to all the pillboxes in the area. We had to cut away all the vegetation along the line of fire and then camouflage the structure itself. I'm sad to see that most of these bits of history have gone but glad that this one at the Haverthwaite-Grizedale junction remains because it was potentially important. We knew of the important prisoners at Grizedale and that there might be Commando-like raids to release them.'

The most northerly pillbox, one of a network protecting the airfield at Kirkbride.

Pillboxes have always fascinated me and nobody prevented youngsters from exploring the insides. The situation today with health and safety regulations would be to board them up or demolish them altogether. I used to think that all pillboxes were alike but I have recently discovered that there were many different designs, each indicated by a government number and varied in shape according to the layout of the land and the positions of vital road or rail links and of course river crossings. There is a fine example still standing and set on a hill overlooking Kirkby Lonsdale. It has a clear firing line towards the bridge which carries the A65 road over the river Lune. What is not so obvious is that the pillboxes were arranged in a set order and each was centrally controlled by telephone.

After the war my father's job was that of a sort of time and motions man, timing the rounds of Cumbria's postmen, some on foot and some using bicycles. He was a keen outdoor man and he took me on many of his favourite walks that he discovered whilst at work. I took a great interest in the pillboxes and although I kept as accurate a note as was possible for a ten year old, I do regret not marking the positions of these boxes, many of which have now gone. I do think that those which are left should be properly listed as historic buildings and are just as much a part of our heritage as the Martello towers built as a defence against a Napoleonic invasion from France in the 19th century.

One of my favourite pillboxes is one of a Type 22 built to protect the Kirkbride aerodrome close to the road to Wigton. The aerodrome was laid out in 1938 as an aircraft storage unit but in 1939 it was given a more active role and as the tide of war ebbed the runways were extended to allow the huge American Liberator bombers, rightly called Flying Fortresses, to land. Other slightly damaged aircraft such as Halifaxes, Bostons, Mitchells, Vengeances and Albermarles were flown in for repairs. As late as 1980 the wreckage of an Albermarle was discovered in a disused quarry near Aspatria and sent to the Imperial War Museum.

When I was working in Seattle in 2002 I met Rex King. When he discovered that I was born in the Lake District he asked me if I knew Kirkbride and then went on: 'After the war I worked until I retired for the Boeing aircraft company assembling airframes, but I'll never forget my stay in Kirkbride. I had a typical American sense of humour but I soon got used to the fact that humour was different in Cumberland. One night I was on my own in the pub and an old farmer handed me a pint of warm beer with a froth on top. "Get that dahn thee," he grinned and then asked me my name. When I said Rex King he laughed and said, "Ahv gitten an owd dog called Rex. Canst tha' feet as well as 'im?" I soon learned that Marra was the local name for a friend and I also discovered that the more the

The Albermarles were ideal aircraft for towing gliders. The Russian markings on this one still remain a mystery.

locals insulted you the more they liked you. When I came in to the pub next time the farmer brought Rex with him to see if I 'wanted a feet' and when he left he gave me a pot of rum butter which I was told was a local delicacy and I should spread it on my bread. It was lovely and I suppose I should not ask how he got that through the rationing.'

The next time I met Rex he gave me a photograph taken at the end of the war. It showed an Albermarle but it had Russian markings. He asked me to find out why this was the case but so far I have not unravelled the mystery. The Albermarles were first flown in 1940 and 640 were built. Their main function was to tow gliders. It is highly likely that American troops in Cumbria were practising for the D-Day landings. It is just possible that some aircraft were given to the Russians to make sure that pressure was exerted on two fronts.

Kirkbride was obviously an important airfield, which means that it was given protection and so I return to the subject of pillboxes. There were three boxes and one of these still stands despite the base being disbanded in 1960. It still shows the supports for a Turnbull gun mount, complete with the handle which was used to swivel the gun.

Pillboxes were not just blocks of concrete. They had bricks or stones set in layers, reinforced by wires and cement between each layer. The fortification was completed by a thick outer coat of cement. This kept the limestone quarries in the north-west of England hard at work until this ring of defences was complete.

Through my father's connections I was able to speak to a number of retired postmen and I discovered how well some of the pillboxes were camouflaged. Sid Wilkes and Ted Cowlishaw told me that: 'One looked like a haystack and one looked like a dilapidated old hen house and it also had hens around it. The lads who manned this would not even let the coppers near it or the men who came to try to count the eggs. Another box in a railway siding looked like an old goods wagon. The real triumph was one that looked more like a combine harvester than the real thing.'

Kirkbride was the most northerly of the Cumbrian pillboxes. Defence was very important and it was here that the voluntary services played a major role. When I was a student long after the war I had several long conversations with my godmother, Doris Dickenson. Her father was a missionary in charge of the seamen's mission in the heart of Barrow's dockland. As mentioned previously Doris was the postmistress at an office in Michaelson Road. Neither Doris nor her father had any intention of deserting their posts even though everybody knew that bombing was imminent: 'Dad would say "God's will" every time a bomb exploded but when he was out of earshot I adapted it to "God help us". I also remember the brave lads in the bomb disposal units who evacuated my office before making the weapon safe. My father was not noted for his sense of humour but he laughed for days following a major night of blitz when the lads of the Vickers yard and a team of Norwegian sailors swept away the rubble and marked out a pitch. An international match was played between England and Norway but somebody had painted ADOLF on the ball.'

The Salvation Army behaved like a real army and dived into the thick of the action. I remember Miss, or rather Major, Brewer staying with my cousin Alan Hargreaves in Cobden Street in Dalton. The name Brewer was perhaps unfortunate for a lady who was so much an opponent of the demon drink. Each time a bomb fell she echoed the words of Doris Dickenson and shouted 'God save us all'. This must have worked because both these spinsters survived to live to a ripe old age. When on duty Major Brewer helped to save others by providing succour to the Barrow survivors of the war. She was always invited to family parties and I was posted as a guard to warn of her arrival. This gave enough time for the adults to put away the cards and the money and prepare to gather round the piano. Miss Brewer loved *Fight the good fight* and she also did well with *Roll out the barrel* but the more modern tunes of the day usually defeated her.

I was reminded of the war and Miss Brewer when I was enjoying a different sort of brew in a German beer cellar in 2006. Suddenly the band struck up *Roll out the barrel* and everybody joined in but the words were in English. I was straight back to the family parties with three uncles blowing their Barrow Shipyard instruments, including cornet, trombone and tuba, with great gusto. My German host shouted 'Don't mention the war' and lots of Germans did their version of the John Cleese sketch showing that they knew and loved the British television series. Perhaps we were all drunk but nobody could stop laughing and one guy squeezed ink from a pen onto his upper lip and did a fine imitation of a manic Adolf Hitler. My German friend owns a vineyard and never forgets to tell British visitors that his name is Adolf. He looks at an antiquated grape press and tells them that he has ways of making them talk.

At this point I paused in my writing for more than an hour. I had opened a bottle of chilled white wine, ate a couple of slices of black bread and a German sausage and lifted my glass to salute a more kindly Adolf. At times like this I know that at last the scars of the last war have completely healed!

Evacuees

I have a couple of personal memories of the time when so many children had their lives disrupted by the war and were often separated from their parents. We had to leave our house in the bombed area of Barrow's docklands and move to Askam some six miles away to be nearer to my mother's family. Even at the age of five, the countryside was a much more relaxed place and we were allowed to play outside with just a minimum of supervision. This seemed strange but even stranger was the arrival of a train load of evacuees from the slums of Salford.

These kids were much rougher and tougher than we were and there were lots of fights between the older boys, but even the Salford girls were able to sort out the local boys. The Mancunian accents were very different and some of the children were not very clean. They did not recognise fresh vegetables or fruit and preferred to eat only chips. They condescended to eat fish but only 'weebatteronit'. We had an eight-year-old ginger-headed lad called George, who still wet the bed and kicked out at the cat, because he 'were freetened on it'.

Soon, however, most of the evacuees settled down and George turned out to be cleverer than me and was a really good drawer. After the war he became a draughtsman and worked for the Avro factory in Chadderton near Oldham. Some of the Salford girls had brought up younger brothers and sisters and, with the exception of a few local farmers' daughters, were much more resourceful on the domestic front.

Alan Wilkinson, who is 77 and now lives with his daughter in West London, fondly remembers his days as an evacuee in Cumbria: 'We lived in Salford and I was in the middle of a family of ten. We existed – yes, that's the right word – existed in a small house close to the docks and the bombing. I was packed off with a label round my neck, clutching a parcel of clothes and a gas mask. We were taken to Victoria station where there was, and still is I think, a huge map painted on the wall showing towns with stations in them. We all tried to guess where we were going. I were separated from my brothers and sisters and sad to say I never saw any of them again. I were sent to live with Mr and Mrs Leece near Millom and we worked on

Many evacuees from Salford were sent to the Lake District.

their farm. I could not believe it when I had a bed of my own and we had our meals round a big table. Mr Leece looked after cows and I had never even seen a cow before, never mind learning to get milk out of one and I got kicked a lot while I were learning.

'School was brilliant and I learned a lot and gradually – but only gradually – got to know and like the village children. A lot later on I married a local lass and learned to speak Cumberland but at first I fell madly in love with "Mad Mavis". She also came from Salford but she was ancient. I'll bet she were at least 20 and worked in the Land Army. Everybody knew her as Mad Mavis because she never seemed to stop laughing and to me she had one really good point. She had the same accent as me and yet the villagers accepted her and liked her. She called her local friends "marra" and could tackle owt. She drove a tractor, rode a horse, caught pigs on the run, sheared sheep and kept the local fellas on a tight string. I'll never forget haytime when the strong lads and lasses were allowed to skip school and all got stuck into bringing in the harvest. When all was safely gathered in, as they sing in church, the village had a harvest supper. Even in wartime this was a real feast and always included a mutton hot pot and pickles. I suspect that the local bobby and the butcher winked at each other as they both tucked in to their hot pot.

'At Salford I was always hungry and I once stole a pie from a shop but in the countryside I learned to eat vegetables, fruit and rations with sometimes a bit extra from the farm and I felt like royalty. I have never been back to Salford, never seen my parents again and I've never watched *Coronation Street.* I worked first at Vickers Shipyard as an apprentice fitter and then moved with the company to Weybridge where I worked on airliners. One of my daughters lives near Hounslow and I live with her. There is always the sound of Heathrow aircraft in my ears but that's nowt compared to the bloody bombing in Salford in 1940.'

Alan Wilkinson certainly landed on his feet but not all were so lucky. There was not only disruption caused to children but many adults were also evacuated. These included school-teachers, which was not surprising, but I also discovered my own version of the Nun's Story.

This arose as a result of talking to Hal and Suzie Bagot who own Levens Hall, which is now open to the public and world famous because of its topiary gardens. Suzie Bagot told me: 'Just before the war Levens stood empty and evacuee children were housed in the Hall, many from Newcastle-upon-Tyne. Then Mrs Anne Bagot offered the house to the Sisters of the Sacred Heart in Roehampton. They were a teaching order and being heavily bombed in the London blitz. The sisters accepted this offer, packed in a hurry and travelled overnight by train from London. The house had no electricity and was cold and damp but the nuns did what nuns do – they accepted the Will of God and got on with the job. The sisters worked in local schools around the Kendal area, especially in the Dean Gibson School, and also taught music to the local children at the Hall itself, some of whom reached a very high standard. At Christmas the children were given a party and each child had to perform a piece of music played on the Steinway piano, which was one of the few items of furniture in the Hall at that time. Mother Monica Edwards was also a talented artist and gave one of her paintings as a reward to a hardworking pupil. The nuns had their own priest, who was named by the children as "Father Onion" because of his bald head. Sunday Mass was open house for the local Catholic families.'

Not all my researches have been successful and I have so far failed to locate any pupils who could complete my 'Nun's Story', but even after this book is published I will continue to explore this phase in the history of Cumbria at war.

Levens Hall – a nuns' refuge in the war.

Office workers from the Vickers yard were taken by bus to the safer environment of the Old Iron Works offices at Askam.

I can also clearly recall the arrival of temporary adult refugees in my home village of Askam. The Vickers shipyard offices kept all the work schedules and it was realised it would cause problems if the bombs wrecked this facility. Therefore, they had duplicate paperwork and had to decide where this could be safely stored and yet not be too far from the works. I have mentioned in previous pages the Furnace area of the former ironworks. By 1939 the only surviving building was the ironworks office and this was requisitioned and refurbished by Vickers. The office girls arrived in the morning by bus or train and always gave a cheery wave to the children on their way to school. One girl's father had an orchard and often handed out apples and pears during the season.

Evacuation at any age is obviously a major disruption, but in time of conflict some hardship was inevitable. Many people rolled up their sleeves and got on with whatever had to be done. This was certainly the case with the men of the Home Guard, and their wives who were obliged to see less and less of their menfolk.

The Home Guard

Humour is part and parcel of the British mentality. Anyone who could laugh at Hitler must be an optimist because Adolf was anything but funny. The comedy series *Dad's Army* was and still is a delight to all, but there was also a very serious and important aspect to what was a surprisingly well trained organisation.

On 14th May 1940 the war minister, Anthony Eden, broadcast on radio to ask men between 17 and 65, even and especially if they had important jobs in industry, to join what he called the 'Local Defence Volunteers' (LDV). He was so inundated that the local police stations ran out of recruitment forms. Recruiting officers were very elastic in their age limitations and some men did excellent work whilst in their active eighties. The Local Defence Volunteers soon became victims of the aforementioned sense of humour and were renamed *Look, Duck and Vanish*. No doubt Winston Churchill smiled, but he insisted on the name being changed to the Home Guard. The Germans tried to stop this by broadcasting an item to the effect that all members of the Home Guard would be shot when the Nazi invasion was successful. This worked, but only to lengthen the queues of men wanting to join.

Joan Hibbert has a very important recollection of the Home Guard's operations in Cumbria: 'I remember when I was about ten, early in 1940, I was walking with my father around Windermere. Suddenly two lorries and a posh car turned up and out got what turned out to be Home Guard men and very official people carrying cameras. They took pictures of the soldiers jumping in and out of boats along the shallow edges of the lake and as they ran smoke bombs were let off to simulate

The Home Guard were a surprisingly versatile force. These men were landing from a motorboat on the banks of Windermere during an exercise.

a battle. Another lot were photographing Home Guard men on speedboats pointing machine guns at the supposed enemy. I often wonder what they used the photographs for.'

Of course one can never be sure but it seems that these photographs were used in the published Home Guard Manuals. Geoff Cain, now in his eighties and still going strong, takes up the story: 'I'm one of those people who like to keep things neat and tidy. I have always kept a diary and my wartime notes show how busy I was working in the Barrow shipyard and doing my Home Guard duty after work. I always took care to keep my Home Guard uniform in order. We were all proud to have this because all we had at the beginning was a LDV armband which we made ourselves. I still have the books I bought including the *Home Guard Manual of 1941* and *Britain's Home Guard* by John Brophy. This has a picture of the huge, 6 feet 5 inches Sergeant Major Bill Waters, who we all loved. There were also photographs of Home Guard units operating around Windermere but I expect these were posed photographs.'

Indeed they were and it seems certain that Joan Hibbert saw these being taken.

I don't think that many people know that the Barrow Home Guard, or rather one member of it, played such a vital role in the recruitment of the Home Guard. When I recently visited the Dock Museum at Barrow I met Graham Cubbin, who gave me the story behind the painting used in the Home Guard Manual: 'It was the work of the war artist Eric Hemmington. It shows Bill Waters, a veteran of the first war, doing a spot of fire watching around the cranes of the Vickers shipyard. The big man's features did quite a lot I think to instil confidence at a time when things were not going well.'

Geoff Cain supports this view: 'Oh yes, as I've said, the Sergeant Major was a huge fella with a big grin and we thought that we could not lose the war. We had more respect for Big Bill than for the officers who commanded us and the Sergeant Major's word was law.'

Bill Waters – symbol of a fighting spirit.

What has emerged from my researches on the Home Guard is that it did follow the army pattern in having specialist units and this was certainly the case in Cumbria. For example, men past the first flush of youth were not just drafted in to do so-called normal duties. There was at least one unit made up of troops mounted on horses and they learned to ride without saddles so that they could react even more quickly. Another unit consisted of men who owned motorcycles and used their own machines, such as Royal Enfields, Nortons and BSAs. They were to function as despatch riders in the event of an invasion.

Communications were obviously vital if there was to be any coordinated reaction to enemy troop movements. This led me to talk to Josie Fitzsimmons who had a very strange memory of my father: 'My grandad were not freetened of owt except your dad. It happened like this. He were 76 when the war started and had served in the first war. They turned him down because of age but soon after your dad turned up with a plain clothes policeman. The three of 'em went into the hut where the old man kept his pigeons and as they went there my mum noticed that the old chap were really freetened. He were alreet when he came out and soon after a telephone were put in our house and extra food arrived for the pigeons.'

I knew that at the start of the war my father's post office training led him to being drafted in to study how an invasion needed to be plotted in the north-west of England. Telephones were vital but if these were cut a few radio sets were made available and pigeons could be used. Dad also had to map out all the breeding sites of the peregrine falcons which kill birds in flight, including pigeons. Just before he died I at last persuaded my dad to talk about his communications role and typical of this was: 'The pigeons would have been a last resort and I was pleased when I used to take you on a tour of Cumbrian peregrine nest sites knowing that nobody had to shoot them. I have lots of happy memories of the war and am delighted that people at that time could work hard and also play hard.'

No account of the Home Guard can ever be complete

The Home Guard parading near Alston.

without reference to the so-called 'special units' whose activities were so secret that it is not easy to unravel them even to this day.

The special units signed and strictly adhered to the Official Secrets Act and each unit was composed of only six or eight men under the control of a local dignitary, who was given the honorary rank of major. These units were trained as well, if not better, than front line troops, given the very best equipment and then told to carry on with their normal civilian tasks. Each unit had a secret underground den very carefully camouflaged and containing weapons and rations to last for a week. If invasion came then they were to hole up and emerge to carry out sabotage operations to disrupt all enemy movements. It was not expected that the units would survive for very long but they would delay the enemy long enough for larger units to head for the hills and continue the war from there.

The men of these units were selected with great care and consisted of poachers, fell runners and skilled hill workers. Messages were to be passed by young girls pretending to be out horse-riding and the prettier they were, the less likely the Germans would be to shoot them!

Chapter 5

Work and Play

'**Work hard and play hard' is a phrase** often used these days but this was much more necessary during the war years – that is, if there was anything to play with. These days people sit for hours by their televisions or computers and yet the young complain that they are bored. They would certainly not have been happy with the entertainment on offer in Cumbria during the war. People in those days made the best of what they had in conditions which locals described as a 'bit of a rum do'.

Some houses had a piano and many more had a wind-up gramophone although the metal needles were in short supply as wartime restrictions came into force. Tunes like *Roll out the barrel*, *Run rabbit run* and *Underneath the arches* were played until worn out and the latest Vera Lynn blockbuster was a treasured item. Sheet music was preserved like leaves from the family Bible and singsongs 'around the old Joanna' were features of many parties. Music had to be the food of love because 'proper food' was very much in short supply as rationing started to bite.

Brass bands were more than welcome and often toured the towns and villages, stopping and playing tunes at each corner. Whilst the young men were at war the old chaps tried to blow an instrument rather than a gasket! Dance bands were booked up weeks in advance and many members of these were from the Salvation Army and were more used to hymns rather than Hims and Hers dancing 'too close for comfort'.

It was the cinema, then called 'filums', which was the major lifeline for folk who wanted escapism and Charlie Chaplin's *Great Dictator* put Adolf Hitler in a much more enjoyable light. Initially the Government decided to close theatres and cinemas but soon realised that this was a mistake and changed their minds. Every village had its own picture house and towns had several, varying in style from palatial establishments to the well-named 'flea pits'. These were so very different to the modern complexes and so was the atmosphere within them.

'Gone with the Wind' was more like 'Come with the Smoke' as the projector's beam penetrated the stygian gloom of tobacco fumes. In those days almost everybody smoked and most people smoked very heavily indeed. The equipment in cinemas was not always reliable and there would be frequent breaks as bulbs had to be replaced or snapped film cobbled together and re-threaded.

Because of the obvious transport restrictions villagers in Cumbria had to make careful plans to visit a cinema in a town. They had to consult timetables and hope that the last bus was not too full. On the whole it was better to sit on make-shift benches in what was often a shell of a building and hope that the apparatus functioned.

In my home village the Lots Social Club was a case in point. This consisted of a corrugated iron structure lined with driftwood and looking like a large hen hut. When it rained the roof rattled so loudly that it drowned the sound track of the 'filum'. It was heated by a huge coke boiler that became red hot and was protected by a huge home-made fireguard. At times of fuel shortage volunteers went into the local woods and on the beach to obtain wood for the stove. The Lots club was run by Henry Robinson who was affectionately known as 'Tin Bum'. Henry had been injured in a delicate spot during the first war and was manager of the local Co-op. Henry did a wonderful job for everybody by keeping the Lots Social Club going all through the war and beyond and was ably assisted by William Woods, his son-in-law. Apart from the weekly cinema show Henry obtained snooker and table tennis tables and had a regular delivery of crisps and Marshes mineral waters. To the village, 'Tin Bum' was a 'Man of Gold'.

Stories of enterprising entertainments are many and various in the Lake District. Between Haverthwaite and Holker a cinema performance was disrupted by a flock of sheep gaining forcible entry by one door and going out through another. This diversion would have done credit to a bull in a china shop. Another performance near Sedburgh was disrupted by a flock of aggressive and very loose-bowelled geese, whilst a pig entered a cinema near Millom. Who said that the cinema was not live entertainment?

Children who spent time sitting in air raid shelters listening to bombs falling, perhaps, like me, learned to read by candlelight. Apart from comics like *Dandy*, *Beano* and *Radio Fun*, books were also popular. Sensible parents scoured secondhand bookshops as paper for newly printed books dried up. My own favourite was *Swallows and Amazons* by Arthur Ransome (1884-1967). He spent a lot of time in Coniston and I had a friend at school who had met the great man, who gave him a rod and some hooks whilst both were fishing. I knew that the plot of *Swallows and Amazons* was based around Coniston and, in July 2008, I went aboard a very modern solar-powered boat on a cruise of the lake which focussed on the locations used in the book.

In the summer of 1990 I was invited to attend the opening ceremony of the Ransome Society held in Coniston. There I met and subsequently had conversations with Brigit Altounyan, who told me: 'Arthur loved children and he based his *Swallows*

Brigit Altounyan proudly opening the Ransome Society in the summer of 1990.

and Amazons book around our family. I was called Titty in the book and later he told me that he was so worried in the war that he gave away many copies to children, including evacuees, he had never met before. He told me that in wartime children needed all the help they could get. His own life was full of strife because he had worked as a journalist in Russia after the First War and his second wife was Trotsky's secretary before he was assassinated. Wars and senseless slaughter made him very angry and he had no good word to say about any Fascist leader and especially Hitler. I suppose that he had communist sympathies but towards the end of his life he was a pacifist. Even when he wrote *Swallows and Amazons* in 1930 his only thought was to give pleasure to children.'

I can vouch for the fact that this aim was successful and I still treasure the book itself and the film that was adapted from it.

No account of Cumbria at War should omit this Ransome episode but neither should the works of Beatrix Potter (1866-1943) be forgotten. Her books also gave solace before, during and long after the war. Beatrix was brought up in London and was a well-respected wildlife illustrator working for the Natural History Museum. She was an expert on fungi and she illustrated a book on the subject that was the standard work at that time. For many years I worked for and with the naturalist John Clegg who lived in retirement at Kents Bank near Grange-over-Sands. John was the editor of the 'Wayside and Woodland' series of books published by Frederick Warne. Beatrix illustrated the book on fungi in the series and her children's stories were also published by Warne.

John took up the story when we were working together on another series of books: 'Beatrix made a lot of money from her books and moved to the Lake District which she loved and became an expert sheep farmer. I met her last in the summer of 1942 and she said that the war looked as if it would eventually be won. She actually said that she hoped that the children in the war had not become too nervous to reach for a book. Her final words to me were that the threat of invasion had gone and the Lake District was safe.'

She need not have worried because many children, like me, read by candlelight in the shelter and forgot about Adolf and thought about Mrs Tiggy-Winkle.

How many times in this very sophisticated age do parents spend lots of money on Christmas and birthday presents, especially for young children, only to find the gift ignored and the child playing happily with the box? This surely proves that children can make their own fun and the presents given during the war did not have to be spectacular. The child's imagination is spectacular enough! I still remember my favourite present for the Christmas of 1941 when I was five. It was a Macintosh Red apple and I polished it until it shone and my span of interest continued long after I had eaten it. To this day I still eat the stump of my apples and wait eagerly for the Egremont Russet season which delighted all Cumbrians in the war.

Presents, like beauty, are in the eye of the beholder, as Joyce Bennet recalls: 'My grandfather was 74 when war broke out and he was a joiner and undertaker in Kendal. There were lots of bits of wood, cans of paint and varnish when hostilities began and he was much in demand to make toys for children. He made whips and tops, wooden cradles for dolls, aeroplanes to look like Spitfires and lots of other things. He had a white beard and some of the children were convinced that he was Father Christmas. He tried hard to make Pinocchio puppets with strings on the arms and legs. They actually looked more like garden gnomes. My brother still laughs and says that Grandad invented garden gnomes.'

Jack Simpson has memories of his grandmother who lived in Carlisle and had a dress shop. She spent her spare time making little dresses for dolls made from off-cuts which before the war she would have thrown away. Once clothes rationing started, she had queues of customers bringing old dresses to be cobbled together to make new ones. Her main source of happiness, however, was to provide games and light entertainment for the children in the war.

There were excellent relations between the air force bases at Cark, Barrow and Millom. Christmas parties were held for the children and entertainments at the base were open to local people. ENSA (Entertainments National Service Association or also called 'Every Night Something Awful') also played a part and performed a variety of shows. The station linked into the town by performing shows in Barrow Town Hall and Her Majesty's Theatre. I was five and this was the first time I had been to live theatre. I can still remember being frightened by airmen and women who were dressed up as German bombers covered in blackout sheets and being shot down by very loud 'gunfire'.

Sport has always been a major form of entertainment and there was probably more high quality sport played in Cumbria during the war than in any of the southern counties. Many very fit young men were exempt from call-up to the armed services because they were skilled engineers or mine workers. The typically northern sport of Rugby League was more important in Cumbria than soccer and the games played between Barrow, Whitehaven and Workington were of a very high standard. Even villages could produce a tough and talented 13 on the field plus an impressive waiting list. The games were eagerly supported and provided a welcome relief from the rigours of war. It was no accident that when a team was sent to tour Australia after the war three Barrow-bred lads were selected. On the boat in 1946 were Jimmy Lewthwaite, Willy Horne and 'Ginger' Hughes. Willy went on to captain Great Britain against Australia and won the Ashes. Ginger Hughes produced an even more famous son who for some reason played football. Emlyn Hughes captained both Liverpool and England.

Willy Horne is without doubt the most famous sportsman Cumbria has produced. He could certainly have played cricket as a professional had he not been so successful at Rugby League. He trained as an engine fitter working on submarines from 1937. He told me in the 1980s that he could remember the names of all of the Barrow ships which served in the war. It must have been a surprise when, as a member of the 1946 rugby team to Australia, they travelled aboard the aircraft carrier *Indomitable* which had taken part in the Malta convoys of 1941 and 1942. She was built in Barrow.

One sport unique to the county is hound trailing. This was like a fox hunt except that the hounds followed a trail of aniseed along an obviously marked course well-known to the spectators. This really was an up-hill and down-dale sport. Those who laid the trail were very fit lads and so were the wardens who tracked the hounds to ensure fair play. I still remember the names of some of the hounds, such as Bomber, Fighter and Glider, which was the most successful of them all. The trailers obviously knew the hills very well and some were given secret training in case there was an invasion. Vital

Willy Horne learned his trade in the engine shop of the Vickers shipyard.

Willy the Player, a Cumbrian legend at rugby and cricket.

messages could not be carried across such harsh terrain by motor vehicles, nor indeed by horses. One such hound trailer was a Norman Wharton who lived at Ireleth near Kirkby and had played as goalkeeper for Sheffield United.

Keeping the hounds fed during the war must have been a problem and I knew of one owner who often gave the family meat ration to his best hound. It was thought that he used the hounds' prize money to buy even more meat on the black market and local farmers provided 'rations' for the speedy beast because they had a substantial bet on the success of the hound. If the dog lost, the family went hungry. No wonder one man, his dog, his wife and kids helped to train the animal to a peak of fitness.

As already mentioned, cigarette smoke hovered around each and every group of people be it inside or out. Almost everybody smoked but until the war the idea of women smoking in public was frowned upon. Ivy Corrigan told me: 'I were 18 when the war started and only tarts went alone into pubs and only loose women smoked outside their own houses. Fags were never rationed during the war which is a surprise because each one had to be shipped. There were times when they were in short supply and you could not always choose a particular brand. When I went to work in a munitions factory and was doing a man's job but for less money we decided to smoke, drink beer and play darts. I've never liked any of these but we felt we had to make a point. We were an early sort of women's lib I suppose and God knows it were needed.'

Alan Hargreaves also remembers being shocked as a teenager: 'I remember standing in Tudor Square in Dalton when some factory lasses came along smoking and telling jokes in public. They were behaving like men and it took some getting used to.'

To be honest it also took the government some time to get used to this. When cigarettes were in short supply there was a suggestion to restrict smoking to men only! Commonsense prevailed and if it had not there would have been two wars –

War and Sport – the Barrow-built aircraft carrier Indomitable *took part in Operation Pedestal to bring relief to Malta in 1941. After the war, in 1946, it took the Rugby League Touring Team to Australia.*

War and Sport – in 1946 the Indomitable *provided passage for the Rugby League tourist team to Australia. Four Barrow players included Willy Horne, hidden at the back and Jimmy Lewthwaite (far right). Ginger Hughes is fifth from the left at the front.*

one Britain versus Hitler and the other men versus women. The losers would certainly have been Hitler and men!

It cannot be repeated often enough that the war would not have been won if the women of the country had not rolled up their sleeves. They looked after the children, ran the house, controlled the rations and equally important they filled the vacuum in the working place traditionally filled by men. They became engineers, bus drivers and clippies and even pilots delivering aircraft from factories to operational bases.

They also did what women still do best – they looked after feckless men. Sheila Holmes who now lives in London recalls: 'My mum's friend worked in the NAAFI at Millom camp and told her that the men were well fed and felt sorry for us living off rations. There were a lot of Polish airmen on the camp and as they learned to speak English they would come into the NAAFI. They often passed them a slice of bacon or an egg sandwich to take home to their children. They could not do this as they were sometimes searched as they were going home. What they did was to eat the gift themselves and then give all of their rationed items to the family. She said that the NAAFIs were happy places with some of the men being very musical. The impromptu entertainments were an amusing blend of Anglo-Polish.'

I always think that it is a bit of an insult to treat men and women at work during the war as two separate things when everybody was mucking in together. Two jobs were different, however, mining and quarrying which require lots of training and in those days great physical effort. This meant that the men had to do this job and they were quite rightly not called up to serve in the armed services.

To understand how important mining was in Cumbria all one has to do is to list the essential things needed to win the war. Iron and steel were vital and coal was needed to fuel these industries. There were iron ore mines all around the county. Iron is in everybody's blood but never more so than in ex-iron mining villages, such as Dearham and Cleator Moor, as well as towns like Workington and Millom. Coal mining was for many years the lifeblood of Whitehaven which had coal seams that burrowed deep under the sea.

All these mines were working at full capacity during the war. I had a friend called John Trelore and all of his family worked in either the iron ore or the coal mines. Their families had all moved from Cornwall in the 1870s when the tin mines started to close. So did the Freethys, which is why my surname is not common anywhere except in Cornwall. My paternal grandfather was an iron-ore miner and my father told me something of what life must have been like in the workings during the war. At this time Digging for Victory in Cumbria had two very different meanings.

Milly Jenkinson told me: 'My father-in-law worked in the iron ore mines near Egremont and his two brothers earned their crusts in the Whitehaven coal pits. They had very different safety precautions but they were all tired of trying to meet the essential productivity targets. No coal miner would dream of allowing a naked flame in the pit because the build-up of methane gas would result in lethal explosions. More miners are killed by gas explosions than from any other cause. The iron-ore miners could have a bonfire down below if they wished because methane was not present in this environment. When they came home the coal lads were black and the men of iron were a rusty red. Both the coal and iron mines were hard at work in the war to feed the greedy iron and steelworks, especially those in the Workington, Millom and Barrow areas. The Hodbarrow iron-ore mine near Millom has now been flooded and landscaped and is a splendid nature reserve. What gave work to my ancestors is now giving pleasure to the next generation.'

These days Cumbria is regarded as a rural county and earns its living from tourism but this is a recent event. The whole area sits on top of huge deposits of coal and iron ore. Apart from the ironworks in the big towns like Barrow and Workington, there were smaller but still important works in places like Ulverston. Just after the war – in 1946 – the Ulverston ironworks was demolished and on the site the Glaxo Company developed a much more sterile product. They made penicillin and streptomycin which saved so many lives. The secret work went on during the war and the many injured men dying of septicaemia were a great incentive to develop drugs.

Still on the subject of iron and steel, I had an interesting conversation some years ago with Bill Ousby, who lived in Gleaston on the road between Ulverston and Barrow: 'When you write about iron foundries, don't forget to mention that blast furnaces can't function without limestone. There was a huge quarry at Stainton close to where I live and there were other workings in the quarries in the Penrith area that provided the raw materials for iron works around Workington.'

The iron ore of Cumbria was of such high quality that it accounts to a major extent for the development of Barrow as a major ship building centre. Cumbrian ore, especially from Hodbarrow which only closed in 1968, and the metal produced from it was preferred by such prestigious customers as Rolls-Royce.

Many rail links led to the huge steel works and from there to the shipyard. Once processed, iron ore and steel were transported by ship especially from the docks at Workington, Maryport and Millom. Maryport now attracts more and more visitors and the marina is considered to be one of the best in the north-west and is always full of pleasure craft. The line of the old railway line to the docks can still be seen and Maryport's strategic importance was known to the German 'tourists' of the 1930s.

The same situation applied to the larger town of Whitehaven, built and designed to suit the needs of Georgian England from the 1780s. Later on large deposits of coal and iron ore were found and the port began to export these assets whilst continuing to import timber but especially tobacco and rum from the West Indies.

I must admit that I have always had an affection for Whitehaven, which is now secure on the tourist map with memories of the old mines and of the history of rum. In the 1930s, however, the only visitors were the German 'tourists' and they also visited and photographed 'Wukington'

(Workington) which was a mining town full of guts and grit. During the war, there were detailed Luftwaffe maps showing the dock installations in these areas. The 'tourist spies' had certainly done their work well. Many of the miners knew at least something about the German invasion plans and a few men were selected to blow up mines and installations to prevent the enemy from using them. There was also a select band of local quarrymen who were sworn to secrecy but were well prepared to hinder the activities of any occupying force.

Alan Bowker was one of those who remembers something of these plans: 'I were a young quarryman at Shap when a fella in a posh suit came – I think it were October 1939 – and he sat down among us. He spoke to the young fit lads who could run up and down the fells. Without telling us why, we were told how to read a map and identify mine shafts and quarries dug years ago by the Old Man. This was a term used to describe old miners and there were a lot of these on Coniston Old Man which is how it gets its name. My father were a shot firer, which meant he knew how to place explosives in holes which him and his mate had drilled. He were then sent to Workington and joined up with other quarrymen and miners. They were told how to blow up railways, roads, docks and buildings. Our quarry manager told us to keep quiet about what the man in the suit had told us to do and to get on with our normal jobs until he told us that trouble were brewing. We all noticed that he were given a brand new safe and only the manager had the key which he kept tied to his watch chain. We never saw the chap in his neat suit or his posh car again but no doubt he were briefing other quarry chaps.'

In the summer of 2008 I spent some time with Gordon Angus, who helps to run the Thelkeld Mining Museum near Keswick. We were both surprised that this granite quarry was closed for the duration of the war. He told me: 'This is a huge quarry and it was fenced off in 1939 and guards were placed on it. Local folk said it was to store essential rations in the event of an invasion but it now seems certain that here were secret armament dumps needed to repel invasion. After all, what is the point of saving tons of rations which could easily be captured by an enemy? Just look at this quarry – it is huge, with lots of places to preserve high explosives in caves which can still be seen today. The secrets have still not been totally unravelled.'

People did not just think about the war effort when they were at work but clearly this was uppermost in people's minds. It was obvious that metals were scarce and old materials had to be collected and recycled. Norma Sykes clearly remembers this aspect of the war: 'I was at school in Appleby and there were a poster on the wall asking our parents to give up old and unused cooking utensils. I remember not being pleased when the photograph on the poster showed only lads but all my elder brothers did was laugh. We all wrote down the rhyme which

A boy-dominated Pots and Pans Collection advertisement!

Collecting pots and pans. Did they go to make aeroplanes or was it just a publicity stunt?

our teacher set to music. I can still remember the words to this day:

My saucepans have all been surrendered
The teapot has gone from the hob
The colanders leaving the cabbage
For a very much different job.
So now when I hear on the wireless
Of Hurricanes showing their metal
I see in a vision before me
A Dornier chased by a kettle.

Mrs M. Pickering, now living in retirement in Burnley, remembers her teenage years in Sedburgh during the war: 'The old timers like me are fading away far too fast and I'm glad to record my memories when we all had to "make do and mend" and also to follow the rule of "waste not want not". It were my generation who invented the idea of recycling. We were round collecting pots and pans which we all thought would be converted into Spitfires to shoot down Germans. We also learned to find food for free in the hedgerows and knew which plants were good for you before the Health Service was set up. My mum told me to go out and find what she called "Free Food-Edibles and Medicals". If we want lessons on recycling, we could not do better than go back 70 years.'

Chapter 6

Dig For Victory

As I planned this chapter the cost of food was rising and the government was imploring us not to waste food and even grow our own. To those who remember the war this has a familiar ring to it. These days rationing is mainly by price but during the war prices were controlled and it was availability which was the problem. Many of the people who responded to my request for information made the point that most of the poorer people had a better diet during the period of rationing than they had either before or after the conflict.

I have kept a diary since I was at school and one of my entries for 1952 has a reference to rationing during the war because my language teacher arranged for the class to have French pen-friends and she insisted on us describing real events. Instead of waffling on about your auntie having a pen or a cat which sat only on mats we were asked to describe what we ate in the war. We had to compare our food, which was sometimes sumptuous compared to what the Germans allowed the French children to eat.

Country children like me had long learned to live off the land or from the sea. I remember having what we called a 'bank line', which I shared with my friend George Hughes. We both lived within 200 yards of the sea and our line was on the beach. It consisted of a long length of stout string strung between wooden poles. Along the string dangled lots of hooks which we baited with lugworms. We waited for the tide to come in and as it ebbed we followed the water until the bank line appeared. We then collected our catch, which always consisted of flat fish but occasionally small cod or a fine sea bass. There was almost always enough for a couple of family meals and more often than not there was more than we could eat. In the days when nobody had freezers or fridges we went on our bikes and toured local farms to engage in friendly barter. Butter, cheese, eggs and a slice or two of bacon would appear as if by magic and be wrapped up in such a way that even experts in military intelligence would be hard pressed to unravel.

In 1952 my mother worked in an egg packing factory on the Ellers in Ulverston and her job was to look at eggs under a strong lamp to ensure that they did not contain developing chicks and could not therefore be sold. Working with my mother were Mary Phee, who came from Eskmeals, and Edith Case from Bouth.

In the case of Mary, I had to try hard to translate her dialect but it was always well worth it. She told me: 'Me awld fella did not tek to food inspecters nor bobbies durin' t'war. When they cumed to count t'number o' 'ens, sheeps, cows or pigs to mek sur nobody git mo-or than t'ration dad were ready for 'um. They had posh suits and he did nut give a row of sheep shite for any on 'um. He alus kept the cow sheds and yard mucky whenever they was cumin'. My brother worked at gun range i' Eskmeals and you wud not believe the stuff wot got kilt by t'shells. We 'ad to eat all of it afore it went off.'

Edith Case worked in the office and was a more sophisticated lass, who still lives in Bouth. Her memories did not tax my powers of Cumbrian translation. She remembers that: 'Farm children were fed very well because good food was always at hand and so was milk straight from the cow. Our sausages had real meat in them and when some milk went sour it was silly not to convert it into butter and cheese. We had more than 100 hens and some ducks and keeping an account of each and every egg was a problem we did not even try to solve. Local farms would gather together to make sure that all "sickly" lambs did not die together but had phased dying. We all had fields full of

A typical allotment of the 1940s recreated at the Preston Museum.

vegetables for ourselves, our livestock and could sell the surplus.'

Feeding poultry was not a problem in country districts but in some areas they were short of grit. A sort of barter system operated with folks from the coast ferrying crushed seashells to provide the grit and also piles of seaweed were carried by horse and cart to upland areas and spread on the land as fertiliser.

Some coastal villagers made an extra income by pulling seaweed from the rocks, putting it in sacks and taking it to the nearest railway station. From there it was sent off to be processed into agar. This jelly-like substance is still used as a base for cosmetics, toothpaste, ice cream but especially as a sterile medium in which to prepare bacterial cultures. The Glaxo laboratories at Ulverston produced penicillin in large quantities just after the war as well as other microbiological preparations.

Good and reliable medicine was always a problem in the war

and there was also a lack of Vitamin C which was obtained from oranges imported from overseas. This deficiency was countered by the production of Delrosa, which is still on the market today and also known as rose hip syrup. It is easy to make at home simply using sugar (or honey) boiled up with rose hips. Village children in Cumbria were asked to collect hips and take them to school. There they were weighed and one shiny new three-penny piece was paid for each pound. It was worth the scratches and the odd spot of blood when picking the fruit from the thorns. I once collected 13 pounds in one weekend. Growing on the sand dunes were lots of Burnet roses which produce black rather than red fruits. These were richer in Vitamin C, but the low bushes had many more prickles. The bounty for this work was an extra penny per pound and I soon became an expert at finding the best locations which I kept secret for 'economic reasons'. How rich I felt to be earning a living at the age of eight. How is this for child labour?

These aspects of life in the war in Cumbria were minor problems compared with the discipline needed to cope with the rigours of rationing. When I was working the rough draft of this chapter my wife as well as converting my handwriting into print was good at providing mid-morning snacks. It is worthwhile writing down the gist of one of our conversations.

'Can I have a bacon sandwich and a brew?'

'No.'

'OK, so we have no bacon, I'll have cheese.'

'No.'

'What's up? Do we need to go shopping?'

'No. You are writing about the War in Cumbria so I've been measuring your rations. You had two eggs for breakfast and if you are true to the book that's your lot for two weeks. Oh – and another thing – you have had enough butter and cheese in one day to last you for a week. And we've run out of tea and sugar.'

'OK then,' was my final comment, 'let's go to the fish and chip shop for lunch. At least that wasn't rationed.'

'There's some in the fridge,' she laughed and then fed me properly, but she had brought me down to the crux of the problems caused by rationing.

A useful exercise for those reading this section of the book would be to list the weekly ration, then go and do your weekly shopping and compare the two. Ada Gunson gave me the idea when she contacted me regarding rationing in Millom: 'Before I rang you I measured out a weekly ration but as I remember it quantities did vary according to availability. On my kitchen table I laid out the portions and waited for my three grandchildren to arrive with my daughter-in-law. I had 12 ounces of sugar, 4 ounces of butter, 4 ounces of bacon, 2 ounces of tea and an egg. I also weighed out half a pound of meat and two sausages. We then went to do the weekly shopping but I told them all to stick to the basics. Even I were shocked when I saw how much we all ate. There were fat kids in the war but not many. Those who were fat were fat because of their natural make up and not from eating too much. I feel sorry for some kids today when they are told that they are clinically obese when some folk are naturally plump. My husband were big enough to play as a front row rugby prop forward and he were fat, but he ate less than me and I'm thin as a lath. My five-year-old granddaughter looked at my egg for the week and said, "Thank you for beating Hitler, Grandma". As I was only seven when war broke out I was pleased to have played such a vital part in the Victory.'

I showed Ada's memory to my own ten-year-old grandson who lives in Yorkshire and he told me that he had just finished a project at school and was told that even babies had ration books. This was quite true and there were ration books of different colours. A green book enabled pregnant women and children under five to go to the front of the queue and to have priority if fruit became available, they could have two eggs and not one and an extra pint of milk. Children between 5 and 16 had a blue ration book and could have an extra pint of milk but only if it was available. The rest of the population had a

BETTER POT-LUCK
with Churchill today
THAN HUMBLE PIE
under Hitler tomorrow
DON'T WASTE FOOD!

buff-coloured ration book and the coupons within were carefully scrutinised and the cut-out coupons had to be accounted for by the registered shops.

'These inspectors were chaps in training to be Hitlers,' Dora Myerscough, who worked at the Maypole grocers in Dalton during the war, told me. 'They would turn up suddenly and demand to see the coupons which we kept in a drawer. They also carried their own weighing scales to ensure that rations were being measured properly and every customer got the correct weights.'

Jack Small, who was a grocer near Ancaster Street in Barrow docklands, did tell me that there were people who cheated but after the war, when rationing stopped, people voted with their feet and the cheats went out of business.

Jed Cooper, who farmed near Carlisle, told me of another unpopular aspect of some of the food inspector's work: 'Some of the buggers even watched us milking cows or pullin' eggs from under t 'ends to mek sure each squeeze of milk and every egg were noted. I confused one on 'em one day when he looked under my bantams an' I cud see 'im wukkin' owt how to record li'le eggs. In the end he gived up being nossey and we 'et the eggs.'

Village people were encouraged to keep a pig but these had to be licensed and the local police, who were normally friendly with the locals, had the unenviable job of supervising what became known as 'pig clubs'. The clubs, however, were crafty and hid a beast or two away from prying eyes. On the hills between Ireleth and Dalton lived one pig called 'Skit', named after the local police sergeant. Those who helped to feed the illicit pig and the local butcher who killed the beast were given a cut of meat which was delivered under the cover of darkness.

When I asked for listeners' memories on my slot on BBC Radio Cumbria in June 2008 I had a fascinating call from Mary Briggs, who is 89 and still going strong. She said: 'Look lad, you need to put summat reet. I watch too much telly 'cos of mi bad legs and there were a programme on about rationing in the war. It med fun of it as if it were not an important subject. We had our fun even in the worst of times but we measured our rations carefully. We had not much money but were better off than in the 1930s when we had nowt on most days. In 1941 I were pregnant with our first child and my husband had just gone away to war. What were good about rationing, at least we knew we could afford it and greedy folk could not buy everything in the shop. My husband sent me money regular and the neighbours were brilliant in them days. It were not so much of "Make do and mend" as "Make do and lend". Clothes appeared for the baby and when she had grown out of 'em they were washed, mended and given to somebody else. Vegetables appeared on my doorstep and I never knew who had sent 'em. Two eggs and a pint of milk appeared on the step when I opened the door one morning and I knew it was my little lass's first birthday. These days too many young folk don't even know their neighbours but in the war we all mucked in together. When I'm one hundred I'll write to the Queen and ask her how much she remembers of the war.'

Later on in the same day Olive Crossland rang me: 'I were ten when the war started and I were the youngest of five and my four brothers and father worked down the Whitehaven coal mines. Very few parents in our street could read or write very well and I never saw my dad put pen to paper except to print his betting slip. I don't think the postman ever came to our house except for Christmas and birthdays. Then as the war started there were some'at in the mail each day mostly about rations and gas masks and I had to help my mum to read them. One thing I read was from the Ministry of Food and it told us about something which I still do to this day. The butter ration should be spread thin and eaten with the butter side nearest to your tongue. I later trained as a nurse and I know that most of the taste buds are on the tongue. One thing that everybody learned during the war was never to take food for granted and I still don't. We never had books in our house and I read these Ministry of Food leaflets over and over. Characters like Doctor

Carrot and Potato Pete were my comic heroes. I tried this with my own kids and the result was they ate more vegetables than their friends and made up characters and stories. One of my daughters invented "Turnip Ted", "Cauliflower Colin", and her favourite was "Liza Lettuce".'

I showed Olive's ideas to my grandson and his friends and they were soon hard at work inventing Russell Sprout and Sir Charles Cabbage who was posh and a member of the green party.

Children in rural areas, as in most of what is now Cumbria, were very much into growing more food and it was as much a case of 'Plough for Peace' as 'Dig for Victory'. At this time there were more horses than cars and the noble beasts did not break down so often and neither did they need fuel. With the normal routine merely accelerated and production targets imposed upon them, a farmer's life went on with minimal disruption.

Things changed as more and more food had to be grown at home but it perhaps took occasional visits from the people in urban areas to make rural folk realise that there were going to be serious food shortages unless they did something about it. Audrey Bradley made this point to me: 'The first we heard in Kendal about the seriousness of Dig for Victory was when we were visited by an elderly aunt and uncle who had been bombed out in Manchester. They told us that people who had gardens were planting veg not flowers and that there were community schemes involving digging and planting. There was even one opposite Piccadilly station and there were volunteers on duty to see that nowt was pinched. Waste areas were converted into allotments and some were on areas flattened by bombs. At this time I realised what the "Dig for Victory" and "Don't waste food" were and I asked for my own plot at the back of the farmhouse. I was seven when the war started and to be honest I've never stopped digging since and I still love my vegetable garden. There's nothing so tasty as potatoes prepared straight from earth to pan or the smell and sweet taste of newly picked peas.'

During the war most deliveries, including this one of Jenning's brewery in Cockermouth, relied on horses. As petrol became ever more scarce, this form of transport was increasingly important.

There was one other aspect of the war which changed the whole of England forever, but especially in rural counties like Cumbria. In our more lazy days our car is essential for even the shortest of journeys and the idea of walking or cycling to the shops is not a consideration. For one thing the local corner shops which stocked everything have gone and supermarket shopping is too heavy to carry. The idea of shopping once or twice a day is not an option these days. Most Cumbrians in 1940 took a horse and cart for granted and the youngsters got excited when they saw a car. Collecting car types and numbers was a hobby almost as popular as trainspotting and there were more road junctions than railway stations. In those days a car's registration letters – such as EO for Barrow – denoted the place that the car was registered. My friends and I always knew if a car from some far-flung town was in our area. Adults knew that this meant that some government official to do with the war was on the prowl.

Towns and villages were very different in 1940 and the urban sprawl into the countryside was very much a thing of the future. One aspect of the war that probably did most to link city and town to village communities was the Women's Land Army.

The Land Army

It is no wonder that horses, the faithful beasts of all work, played such a vital part in the economy of the Second World War. Men who had worked with horses all their lives were obviously reluctant to exchange their 'oss for a noisy and smelly tractor. Then came the Land Army girls from towns and cities who were used to petrol and diesel-driven vehicles. They preferred to learn to drive a tractor than to get used to handling a horse.

Margaret Snell, who came from Manchester to Penrith, was able to see both aspects of farming: 'Learning to plough with a

A familiar scene in the Lake District and Lancashire during the war years was a combination of steam traction and horses ensuring that the harvest of hay was brought in, although obviously very labour intensive. This photograph shows men at work – they soon had to be assisted by women.

tractor was not easy because two lots of machinery had to be mastered and keeping a plough straight was the more difficult of the two. When I asked the ploughman with his horse to help he grinned and said, "All I 'ass to do is to laugh. The 'oss knows where to go 'cos 'ees bin atit fer years." This made me realise that a ploughman and his horse were a team and a tractor and its driver were a team but a tractor had no intelligence whatever. I learned to plough with a horse and what a happy time we both had for more than three years. I married a farmer and our kids preferred a horse to a tractor but this is not the case with my grandchildren. They prefer a machine which only has to be switched on and off and does not need grooming or feeding.'

These days we are all used to supermarkets and the idea of mobile shops touring the streets is almost unheard of. In some parts of Cumbria, including Hawkshead, there are still butchers and fishmongers with vans who are prepared to tour small villages and are very much welcomed, especially by the elderly people who do not have cars or a regular rural bus service. Cumbria in the war measured the food travelled not by means of its carbon footprint but by the environmental impact of a horse's hoof print! Onions often travelled less than two miles, tomatoes usually even less and asparagus was grown in coastal areas where there was lots of sandy soil and did not come in a plastic container from Peru. What must be admitted, however, is that locally grown crops were seasonal and tomatoes and asparagus were available for a limited time. Potatoes and onions could be kept for long periods if they could be stored properly and even apples kept well if they were wrapped up in paper or cloth. The milk ration arrived by horse and cart, a contrivance which rattled when it moved. This was because of the measuring cans which hung from hooks on the cart. The milk was dispensed via a tap at the base of a huge churn and measured out. The customer's milk was then poured into their own jug.

Old timers in the villages of the Furness district will

remember Bob Gillbanks who limped along with his horse and cart loaded with seasonal fruit and vegetables. Bob's voice calling 'Now you potato buyers come and get your bait' was familiar to many and so was his horse who always knew the best places to stop. These were at the houses of villagers who bought carrots and gave one to the horse, called 'Billy'. People in those days did not use bags but carried their purchases loose in wicker baskets called 'swills with 'andles' which were made of woven willow by a local craftsman called Will Everitt. Bob Gillbanks was a good businessman in his own way but he deserved it because he was out in all weathers and was shouting to his potato buyers having battled through the snow during the winters of 1940 and 1941. He would always buy surplus vegetables from those with big gardens or from farms.

Four years ago I met Elsie Backhouse when she and her husband were on holiday in Egypt. She recognised my voice from work I was doing on the radio and as we talked she mentioned my home village and Bob Gillbanks: 'Oh ay, I remember old limping Bob from the days when I was in the Land Army. I joined in 1938 and moved to your spot after training. I lived in Bolton and what a difference it were when I came t'lakes. The air I breathed felt as if it had never been used before. What a change from the cotton mills of Bolton. We were given a uniform of a green jumper and breeches of rough brown tweed. I went to Millom Air Museum last year and they have a model of a Land Army girl and she looks a lot more glamorous than we ever felt. I loved those days even in winter when it was freezing cold and we had much colder days than we have now. Just look up at this Egyptian sun and it's over 100 degrees but I've just had a good shiver thinking of them Lake District winters. What a difference there was to my days in the cotton mill.

'Some of the Land Army girls were posher than me and they were not used to getting up early and working long hours. I was, and on summer days with the sun shining it was a pleasure to be milking very early in the morning and then there was lambing and calving. I was so happy at that time that I was willing to turn my hand to anything. I became very popular with Bob Airey the farmer because I'd worked on cotton spinning machines and was not scared of engines or owt. My dad had taught me to use spanners and to listen for faults in engines. I would have willingly worked for ever in the Land Army but after the war I went back to the mill for a while but it drove me mad. My future husband had a market garden and we ran this until we retired only two years ago when I were 86. The war was a lousy thing but it got me out of the mill and taught me that at least fresh air is free. I'm sure this has kept me healthy for all these years.'

What has been fascinating about all the comments made by the ladies who toiled in the Land Army is that not one was negative. They all loved being close to the earth, the plants, the animals, and even the agricultural machines. What I did not know is the Land Army resulted in the formation of another band of wonderful women. I found this out in the summer of 2008 when I met Betty Kirkland who is now aged 87 and living in the village of Satterthwaite close to Grizedale Forest where she worked. She still refers to herself as the 'Lady with the Axe'.

'I was seventeen when the war started and I wanted to follow my brother's example and join the Navy but I was two young to join the Wrens. Instead it was suggested that I joined the Women's Land Army and this I did. I mentioned that I wanted to work on the land but not on a farm and I mentioned that I had been using an axe to chop wood since I was eight. My mother was widowed when I was two and I earned a few coppers chopping kindling for a wood merchant whose family lived next door. Because of this I was then drafted into what was initially an offshoot of the Land Army but in 1942 became known as the Timber Corps. We had a lovely reunion in 1992 but by then there were not so many of us left and we have lost a lot more friends since. I still have the big axe that I used all those years ago.'

At this point Betty produced the axe and the frail-looking, tiny lady went into her garden and used the well-worn 'weapon' to split logs for her fire. She carried three of them in her arms and put them on the fire before continuing:

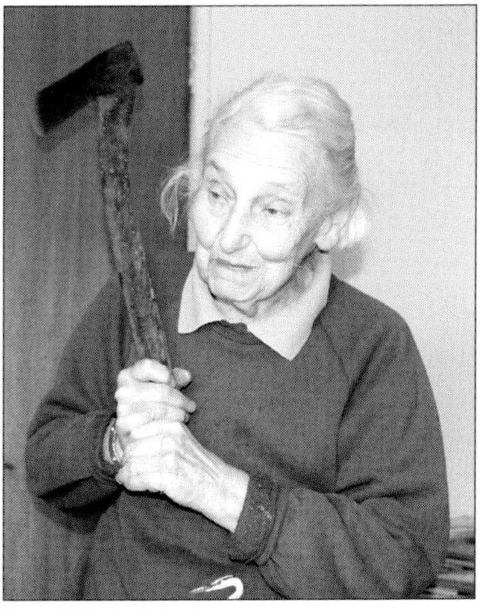

Betty Kirkland poses with her axe in 2008.

'We were given six weeks' training in the Forest of Dean and were taught tree planting and felling by a sprightly young man of 80. He told us that he had to teach us in six weeks what he had learned in more than 60 years. Some of the girls had not been out of the city and one girl from London had never seen a cow, a sheep or any farm animal. After training I was sent to Grizedale and worked outside whatever the weather, even during the winters of 1940 and 1941 when it seemed to snow every day. We had a variety of jobs to do and my main task was selecting trees which were suitable for making telegraph poles. We had to cut each tree we selected off at ground level so as not to waste valuable timber and were told off if we failed to meet these standards. The fallen trunks were moved out of the forest not just by horse and cart but we also had small locomotives which ran on very narrow tracks. I learned to drive one of these engines which was not easy. You had to use your hands to operate the engine and your feet to release a spring which sprayed sand onto the rails to prevent slipping. It was the women who proved better at this job because it seems that we had better co-ordination than some of the big strong lads who were built more for strength than dexterity.

'For each year we served we had a stripe sown onto our pullover and for each half year you had a cross. I'm proud of my six stripes and a cross because I enjoyed every minute of my time at Grizedale and that's why I still live so close to the forest. Some of the logs I am burning I might well have planted myself. We were not just loggers but we also planted thousands of trees during the war.

'Some of the lasses in the Land Army and Timber Corps were big and strong but many were posh and glamorous. I'm only five feet nowt and of slim build but you don't need strength to chop down a tree. You need to use your axe at the right angle and think about what you are doing. The same applies even more so when you are using a saw and you soon learn to anticipate where a falling tree will land. It was not all work and no play in those days because we had lots of fun. I lodged at the Eagle's Head pub with the Jackson family. Outside, every night like this felt like a White Christmas. Sometimes we were provided with transport to take us to a dance in the Coronation Hall in Ulverston. This really did help us to combine work with entertainment.'

Once Betty made me realise that from 1942 the Timber Corps had its own individuality, I discovered more and more ladies in Cumbria who were carrying out this essential work. Not only were telegraph poles essential but so were the timber pit props

Cecilia Little, was a srong lass who worked in the Land Army and the Timber Corps.

needed in the mines. One lady who worked in Grizedale is another 86-year-old youngster called Cecilia Little who now lives in Barrow and whose work involved the cutting of props and other supports used in the iron ore mines. Like Betty Kirkland, Cecilia has fond memories of the Eagle's Head pub, of nights out in Hawkshead and Ulverston, the cold winters of the 1940s and how exhausting it could be working in the wind and weather from 8 am to 5.30 pm. Like many of the girls working on the land, Cecilia at 20 had never been away from home before but like Betty she enjoyed every minute of it.

This view was reflected by Winnie Capstick, who spent five years working on a Cumbrian farm carrying out tasks more typical of those normally associated with the Land Army: 'I started work near Cockermouth in 1940 when we were sure that the war was lost. Every siren meant the beginning of the end especially as letters from home in Newcastle mentioned folks being killed in the bombing. Gradually we relaxed and by the end of 1941 there were fewer alarms but more pressure to work harder to feed the hungry. By 1943 we were sure that Hitler were beat and I think that

The Timber Corps, with a local farmer in Grizedale.

made us work harder. Then we were given a real boost. First Italian and then German prisoners of war started to trickle into Moota camp and suddenly they were coming in waves. Prisoners do not come in those numbers if their war is going well. By 1944 we were already starting to celebrate and wonder what peacetime would be like when we returned home to rebuild our lives.'

Chapter 7

Victory at Last

I remember being woken up on VE Day in May 1945 and taken from my bed to the spare ground in the Lots area of Askam which was called the Flat. A huge bonfire was burning and lads were playing football by the light of the fire. The Askam Hotel which overlooked the Flat was opened up and adults were getting drunk as fast as they could. Potatoes were being roasted in the ashes and *Keep the Home Fires Burning* started the impromptu concert. As the alcohol took over, rude songs were sung about the reproductive apparatus of Hitler, Goering, Goebbels and Himmler but nobody cared. We could hear the church bells in the distance but these were soon drowned out by the sound of whistles and football rattles. Somebody produced a megaphone and placed it next to a wind-up gramophone. The Charles Penrose song about the 'Laughing Policeman' persuaded everybody to laugh.

Bob Brocklebank lived in Ulverston but his father worked in the Barrow shipyard: 'I remember the euphoria as the war in Europe ended. I were twelve and we had school parties, went to special church services and there were street parties everywhere and bunting appeared as if by magic. There was singing, dancing and drinking and many adults fell about drunk. It was much later that my elder sister told me that Mum and Dad were glad that it was all over but they had mixed feelings with regard to what would happen next. They both remembered that in the 1930s Dad was more often out of work than in it and Mum had no job at all. During the war dad worked lots of overtime and mum got a job in an armaments factory. Our grandma looked after us. Food prices were kept low and we had a surplus of cash. I noticed an increase in my pocket money but there was less to spend it on. Our parents were worried what would happen when the demand for warlike things dried up and men returned from the forces and took over jobs which women had done for years. Food prices were bound to increase and all this meant that I could see why they were worried.'

John Harwood, who spent his late childhood during the war in Egremont, was also worried that we may well win the war but lose the peace: 'I started work when I was 15 in 1943 and got a job in the Barrow iron and steel works. I had lots of older friends who worked in the Vickers shipyard. We all knew that once the war was over there would be a decline in the number of warships being built but we hoped there would be repair work to keep us all in work for a bit. This would mean that there would still be a demand for our steel, but this would not last for ever. We scanned the pages of the *North West Evening News* and glanced quickly over the victory celebrations to search for any news of new orders for the yard and the knock-on effect which would affect the whole of the area with coal and iron mines, iron and steel works plus other dependent industries including small family firms. The P & O and Orient shipping companies who operated luxurious liners had sadly depleted fleets and other very battered vessels after the war and were anxious to use their compensation to get back into the travel business. The *Orcades* was launched as early as 1947, the *Orsova* in 1952 and then there came orders for very large fuel tankers, especially the ground-breaking *Methane Princess* which was so large that she was constructed in two huge pieces which were then welded together.

'There was even more euphoria when it was decided to build a super cruise liner which was launched in 1959 and named the *Oriana*. We all remembered the *Orama* being sunk off Norway and that the old *Oriana* was scrapped after doing sterling service during the war. We all cheered when other Barrow-built 'O' liners were being built.'

I remember myself being present at this launch of the *Oriana* beating time with three of my uncles blowing away in the shipyard band to celebrate the event. The war seemed a long way off but there was always that worry in everyone's minds. What next?

Things did indeed get eventually tougher throughout Britain but Barrow's expertise in the construction of submarines proved to be a real lifeline as Jimmy Leatherbarrow recalls: 'The threat of another war – this time with Russia – was rumbling on even as the last conflict was coming to an end. Bigger and better subs were needed and Barrow has built more of these vessels for the Royal Navy than all other yards together. We all know this and are proud of it.'

Ernie Whittaker, who was my schoolmaster in the late 1940s and who died at the age of 97, told me of his experiences during the war: 'I was too old to fight and yet just young enough to worry. To begin with nobody wanted to see a German because it would have meant that we had lost the war and been occupied. From 1942 onwards we started to see camps being built to house first Italian prisoners and then from the end of 1943 came more and more Germans. One of my friends taught in Kendal and he told me each time a load of Germans arrived and were seen heading off towards Grizedale they cheered with relief. We knew that this was a large and important camp but how important only emerged later. Another sign that the tide had turned was that we were stopped

A posed photograph of Home Guard units preparing the Grizedale Camp ready for the arrival of high-profile German POWs.

on fewer occasions when I toured the Lakes on my bike. The Fells were open to us all again – mostly – and you know how important fell walking has been to me and I'm glad that some of this has rubbed off on you.'

The Grizedale POW camp was designated as No 1 and for years I wondered why this was so. I later found out that every German prisoner was vetted before being sent to camps all over England. There were so-called 'white prisoners' who were seen to pose no threat. These could be confined in the southern counties. Then there were the 'grey' prisoners, who were not Nazi fanatics but still likely to be disruptive. These were confined in the Midlands well away from the Channel ports. Next came prisoners in the 'black' category and these men were conceived as a real problem and were high-ranking naval and aircrew officers, most of the former being U-boat commanders. They were placed in Camp No 1 at Grizedale.

Betty Kirkland remembers this camp very well: 'We were working in the Forest at Grizedale when we began to realise that something very secret was happening just when we thought that we were winning the war. For a start we were issued with passes and had to book in and out when we went to and came home from work. I had had a camera since I was 16 and suddenly I was not allowed to use it in the forest after they started to build a camp. Now I know why this was necessary. First they erected barbed wire all around Grizedale Hall and there were rumours that secret types of explosives were being developed there. This proved to be false as an army group took charge and the first of many busloads of prisoners

Sergeants at Grizedale Hall, whose job it was to contain high-ranking German prisoners.

started to arrive. They came with the windows blacked out so that they could not see where they were going and one of the drivers told me that they often drove around in circles just to confuse the Germans' sense of direction. The prisoners became known to us as Black Nazis and our lot were blacker than most and we soon realised that here were the most ruthless of the U-boat commanders. Grizedale was renamed by the locals as "Hush Hush Hall" or the "U-Boat Hotel".

'The officer in charge was Peter Claridge, whose family owned the famous hotel in London. There were also regular visits from the Red Cross who came to ensure that the prisoners were well cared for. As I was lodging in the Eagle's Head pub I got to know some of the off-duty guards at the camp. They told us that some of the prisoners had visited the Lake District as "tourists" in the 1930s and one man had worked as a tourist guide. He was obviously a well-trained spy

The Officers' Mess, Grizedale Hall. It is now used by the Forestry Commission as offices.

and knew the area better than the guards. We were soon hard at work cutting down the rhododendron bushes in the area so that escaping prisoners had fewer places to hide. At the end of the war when all the prisoners had long gone, they decided to demolish the Hall around 1960. That was very silly and I asked why they were doing this. They said that the prisoners had carved their initials on the woodwork and the woodwork was ruined. What a tourist attraction this would have made if some of the initials were identified and the Claridges connection explored more fully.'

Fortunately this lack of interest in the hall by some in the Forestry Commission has not been shared by Brian McMullen who works in Grizedale. He has studied its history from the Ice Ages to the present time and has been fascinated by POW Camp No 1: 'It was not until long after the war that full details of the occupants of the Hall were released. We now know that some designated as war criminals were housed in the very "Hush Hush Hall" before being sent to Nuremberg for trial. One of the lawyers at the trial was Norman Birkett, whose family owned a large draper's outfitters in Ulverston. The most famous prisoner of all was Field Marshal Gerd Von Rundstedt. Obviously these prisoners were largely kept in the manner to which they had become accustomed and there were even more inspections made by neutral observers from the Red Cross. There are records here at Grizedale of these observers' reports. We have photographs, no doubt specially set up, but still invaluable, of the camp being constructed and of groups of prisoners gathered around a piano or visiting the kitchens. There are also many photographs showing just how sumptuous the surroundings were.'

On a day of sweeping rain I spent one of many happy afternoons in August 2008 with Brian McMullen who showed me that a few secrets at Grizedale can still be seen. His office used to be the Sergeants' Mess and he unearthed a photograph of the sergeants outside the building. Judging by their number there must have been a very large contingent of troops to guard

Comfort for the 'black classified' German prisoners inside the U-boat Hotel at Grizedale Hall.

the prisoners. On the opposite side of the narrow road is a cottage which was once the Officers' Mess. Despite the rain we then went into the garden and dug around to find a paved floor. This is all that remains of the guards' kitchens and dining room.

The camp was obviously constructed in great secrecy as Betty Kirkland was aware and the electrical work was done by Hartley and Bramhall, the same Barrow-based firm that worked so successfully on the 'Starfish' project described in chapter one. With such high-profile prisoners, the camp was designed to be escape-proof – our equivalent of Colditz – but there were several brave bids for freedom. One prisoner was shot dead whilst attempting to escape but there was a rumour that his fellow inmates contrived this sad event because he was one of the few U-boat commanders who surrendered rather than fighting to the end. The best documented of these escapes, however, was that of Franz Von Werra who later wrote a book called *The One Who Got Away*. Actually he did escape from Grizedale but after several days on the run he was captured and taken to Ulverston police station. He was then sent to Canada and it was from there that the resourceful German made his successful bid for freedom.

Brian McMullen has researched Von Werra at Grizedale very thoroughly: 'He was a real eccentric and we have lots of photographs of him and his aircraft decorated with symbols indicating each of his combat victims. I think that the real soul of the fella is to be seen in a photograph of the pilot being cradled by the lion cub he had as a pet to symbolise his own bravery. Thankfully the scars of war have healed somewhat and we can now visualise Von Werra and our own resourceful and legless Douglas Bader in the same light. I have been in touch with people who knew some of the prisoners in Grizedale. One of these friends sent me a cigarette case made of wood pinched from the oak panelling of the Hall and this is one of my most treasured possessions. The Hall has obviously gone but some of the outbuildings now used as offices and the public café would still be recognised by the prisoners and the guards whose job it was to keep them secure.'

Brian McMullen, with his treasured cigarette case.

Von Werra celebrates his British victims just before he himself was shot down and captured.

When I mentioned this to Geoff Cain, now living in retirement in Penny Bridge near Greenodd, he was able to add something to the Grizedale Hall saga: 'There are front doors on some of the local cottages which are very impressive and came from Grizedale Hall. Reading Von Werra's book, it is possible to locate the wall which he hid behind and to trace the route he took before being recaptured. He also mentions the prisoners waving to the land girls.'

I now wonder if one of the girls the Germans waved to was perhaps Betty Kirkland or Cecilia Little!

In addition to Grizedale No 1 security camp there were others in Cumbria, some of which initially housed Italians who presented no threat and were excellent farm workers. In their case it was not a case of 'Dig for Victory' but 'Dig to get Home'. There was one camp at Low Wood near Haverthwaite and another at Milnthorpe, plus the well-documented Camp

No 103 at Moota near Cockermouth. This is now a garden centre and motel but during the war the camp was constructed on nine acres of land requisitioned from the Lawson family whose home was at Brayton Hall. Thomas Armstrong was commissioned to construct a camp at an estimated cost of £72,000 to hold 1,200 prisoners.

To begin with the prisoners were mostly Italians but by 1944 there were lots of 'white graded' Germans in residence. Ernie Whittaker noticed that the increasing number of Germans was a sign that the war was being won. This must also have been obvious to the Kirkgate group of local historians led by Gloria Edwards based in Cockermouth who have produced an excellent booklet about the Moota Camp. The group discovered that many of the prisoners, especially the Italians, had considerable artistic talents. The Italians were staunch Roman Catholics and they made a wonderful job of decorating their chapel with religious paintings. The Germans also had talent and they made ornaments from pieces of wood and many locals visited Moota and bought these trinkets using cigarettes for currency instead of hard cash.

Moota Camp 1943.

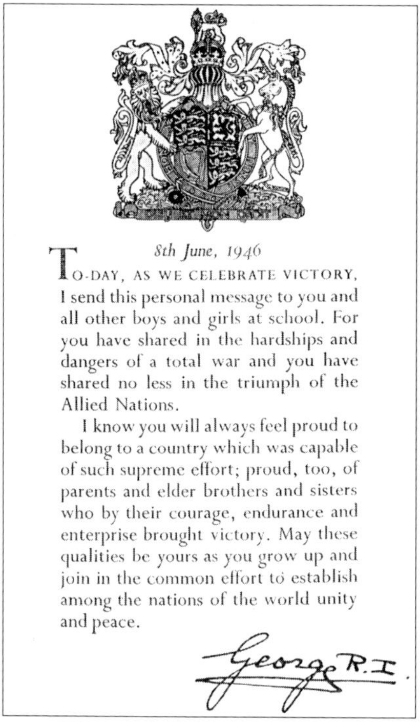

8th June, 1946

TO-DAY, AS WE CELEBRATE VICTORY, I send this personal message to you and all other boys and girls at school. For you have shared in the hardships and dangers of a total war and you have shared no less in the triumph of the Allied Nations.

I know you will always feel proud to belong to a country which was capable of such supreme effort; proud, too, of parents and elder brothers and sisters who by their courage, endurance and enterprise brought victory. May these qualities be yours as you grow up and join in the common effort to establish among the nations of the world unity and peace.

George R.I.

The King's message to schoolchildren celebrating victory, 8 June 1946.

Apart from the most fervent Nazi prisoners, who still believed that Hitler had yet another secret weapon which would win the war, all that the prisoners wanted was an end to the conflict and to be allowed home.

Peace had come but only at a price. People all over Britain and the Commonwealth were prepared to pay this price. This book has, I hope, shown how the people in what is now Cumbria worked hard to win the war and deserved to wave flags, put out bunting, get drunk and party into the night to celebrate. This book celebrates the memories of a declining number of people who stood up to the threat of Adolf Hitler. I have often thought that reunions to celebrate these efforts should be held. I hope that this book may stimulate such efforts.

Index

Other titles on Cumbria from Countryside Books

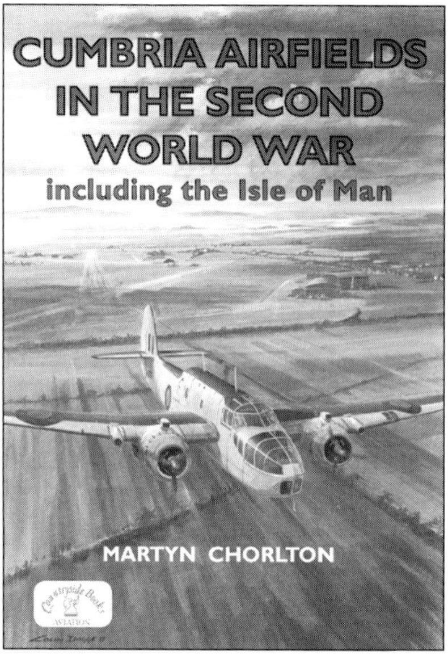